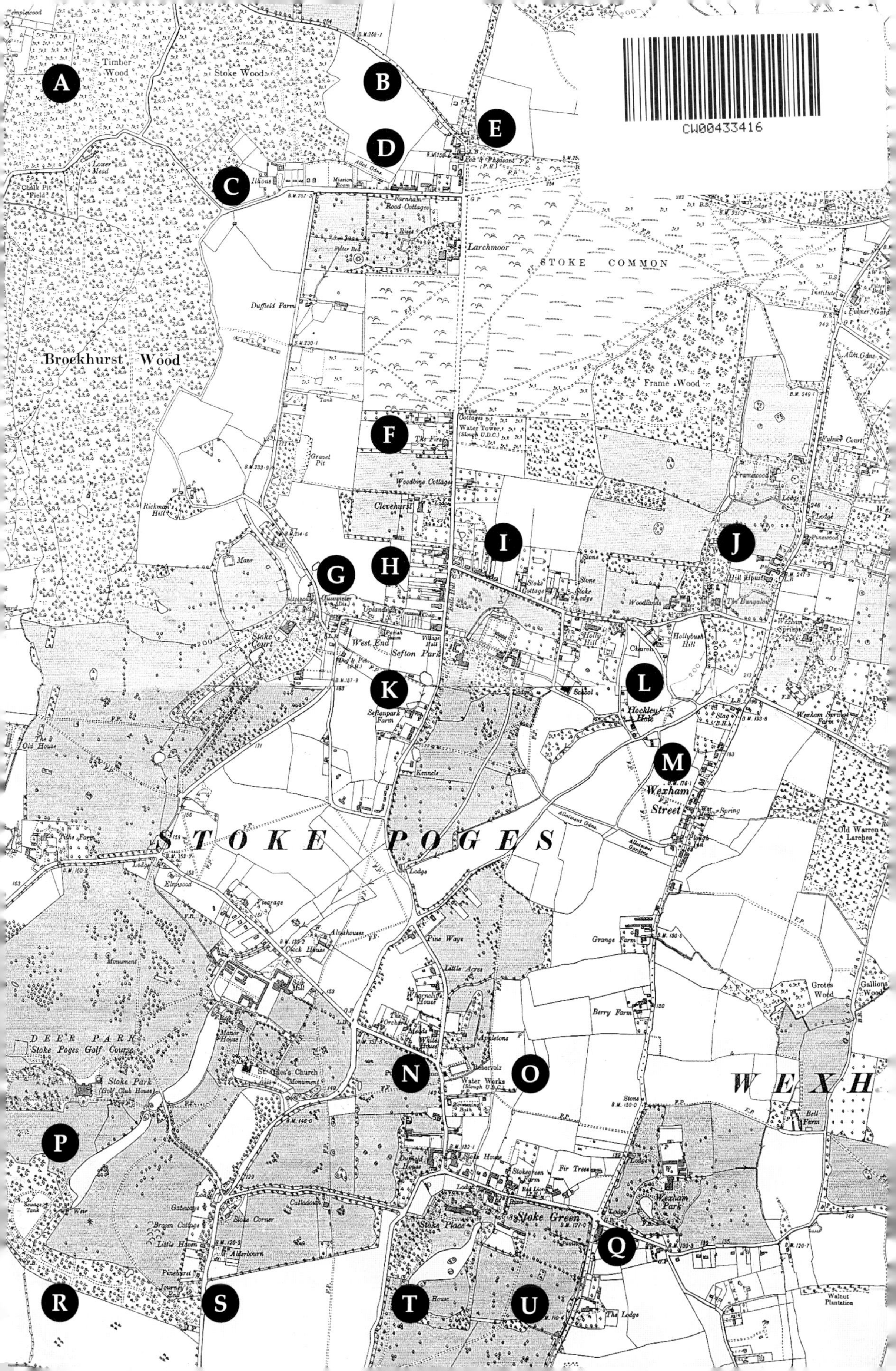

CW00433416
A
B
C
D
E
F
G
H
I
J
K
L
M
N
O
P
Q
R
S
T
U
Timber Wood
Stoke Wood
Lower Mead
Chalk Pit Field
Mission Room
Fox & Pheasant (P.H.)
Farnham Road Cottages
Larchmoor
STOKE COMMON
Institute
Duffield Farm
Brockhurst Wood
Frame Wood
Water Tower (Slough U.D.C.)
The Firs
Gravel Pit
Woodbine Cottages
Clevehurst
Rickman Hill
Framewood
Fulmer Court
Pinewood
Maze
Uplands
Stoke Cottage
Stoke Lodge
Woodlands
Hill House
The Bungalow
Holly Hill
Hollybush Hill
Church
Stoke Court
West End
Sefton Park
Village Hall
School
Hockley Hole
Seftonpark Farm
Kennels
Wexham Street
Wexham Springs
Wexham Springs Farm
Old Warren Larches
Old House
Tithe Farm
Allotment Gardens
STOKE POGES
Lodge
Elmwood
Vicarage
Almshouses
Clock House
Pine Ways
Little Acres
Grange Farm
Monument
Wharncliffe House
The Orchard
White House
Appletons
Berry Farm
Grotes Wood
Gallions Wood
DEER PARK
Stoke Poges Golf Course
Manor House
St. Giles's Church
Stoke Park (Golf Club House)
Reservoir
Water Works (Slough U.D.C.)
WEXH
Bell Farm
Duffield House
Stoke House
Stokegreen Farm
Fir Trees
Wexham Park
Stoke Place
Stoke Green
Gateways
Calladown
Broom Cottage
Stoke Corner
Little Haven
Alderbourn
Pinehurst
Journey's End
The Lodge
Walnut Plantation

Every One A Hero

STOKE POGES IN THE GREAT WAR

Stoke Poges Church, from a postcard of 1911.

Every One A Hero

STOKE POGES IN THE GREAT WAR

Lionel Rigby

Lionel Rigby

Phillimore

2006

Published by
PHILLIMORE & CO. LTD
Shopwyke Manor Barn, Chichester, West Sussex, England
www.phillimore.co.uk

© Lionel Rigby, 2006

ISBN 1-86077-378-8
ISBN 13 978-1-86077-378-5

Printed and bound in Great Britain by
THE CROMWELL PRESS
Trowbridge, Wiltshire

Dedicated to the memory of Sir Nigel Mobbs, KSt.J, JP

Sadly, after writing the Foreword, Sir Nigel Mobbs was taken ill and died on 21 October 2005. The author is greatly indebted to Sir Nigel not only for writing the Foreword but also for his support and encouragement. He and his family have always had a close association with Stoke Poges, and in 1998 he opened an extension to Stoke Poges Village Hall. The men who left the village to go and fight in the Great War would have remembered and used this hall, built in 1912 just two years before the outbreak of hostilities. Sir Nigel appreciated the value of such buildings to the life of a village community. This dedication is our tribute to him.

Contents

List of Illustrations

Frontispiece: Stoke Poges Church, from a postcard of 1911.

Acknowledgements

This book has been written with the generous help of many organisations and individuals and they are listed below. However, I am also indebted to my wife Barbara and to Trevor Harvey, who made extremely helpful suggestions on the structure of the book and contributed his considerable knowledge of the Great War; to Terry Cork whose books and sound advice were invaluable; to Frank Bowater, Ian Huntley and Mac Gollifer for their work on the illustrations in the book; to Naomi Arnold and the Stoke Poges Parish Council and its Heritage Committee for sponsoring the book and especially to Sir Nigel Mobbs who, shortly after writing the Foreword, died in October 2005.

The National Archives
Bucks County Record Office and Family Records Centre
Imperial War Museum
Sir Martin Gilbert
Osprey Publishing
Oxford and Bucks Light Infantry Museum and Dino Lemonofides
Curator, Duke of Cornwall's Light Infantry Museum
Archivists, Coldstream Guards, Irish Guards, Grenadier Guards Museums
Stoke Poges Parochial Church Council
Ian C. Alexander, The War Research Society
Middle Thames Archaeological and Historical Society for John Tarrant's entry to the 'I Remember' Competition
Mrs Mary Wood, the daughter of John Tarrant
Slough Observer
Stoke Poges Threeways Surgery

Rick Albrow, George and Vera Albrow, Marty Alsford, Mrs B.H. Batting, G. Boulain, Patricia Bridges, Susan Burton, Bryan Carter, Penny Cavana, John Chapman, Eric Clark, Eileen Collison, Sheila Cowan, John Cunningham, Kevin Dancer, Gill Evans, Pam Forsyth, Tony Gutteridge, Denis Hartley, Jeanette Hartley, Judith Hassett, Stan James, Les Johnson, Ivor Kilby, Hertford King, Tony Levings, Edna Mayer, Roy Measday, Phil Mills, Mike Milne-Smith, Peter Neville, The Rev. Charles Gilliat Patterson, Andy Plumbly, Thelma Ricketts, Tracie Ricketts, Martin Samson, Jonathan Saunders, Jean Simpson, Dorothy Tack, Kyle Tallet, John Tanner, Pam Trinder, Sue Trinder, David Wood.

We also acknowledge sponsorship of the index by Stoke Park Club and of the Ordnance Survey maps of 1925/6 on the endpapers by Foreman King.

We have made every effort to establish copyright where possible and obtain permission to reproduce, but if we have inadvertently omitted to do so for any particular photograph we offer our sincere apologies. We have also made every reasonable effort to obtain copyright permission for quotations from documents.

Foreword

25 July 2005

Every One a Hero

Anybody who has visited a war cemetery or viewed a village war memorial always wonders who were these ordinary people who sacrificed their lives so that we could live in peace. What were their circumstances; how did their families fare; how did their deaths affect the communities from which they came; and what of those who survived?

For most there are no answers. But in compiling *Every One a Hero* Lionel Rigby has produced a compelling and moving narrative that brings to life the First World War in Stoke Poges in all its poignancy and tragedy. This is an important piece of social history and today, some 90 years later, it is difficult to appreciate the intense emotional pressures that must have affected not only those who served but more particularly their families at home.

Stoke Poges in 1914 was a quiet rural village. Life was organised around the estates of the landed gentry. This is so well described by John Tarrant in his recollection. All this ended on 4 August 1914 and for the next four years many of the young men of the village were, in the spirit of King and Country, involved in the Great War – the war to end all wars.

It is a privilege to look back and read the spontaneous first-hand accounts of trench warfare and death. The book recounts the stories of those who gave their lives and the impact on parents, loved ones and friends. These are stories of gallantry and duty.

In all 48 young men of Stoke Poges fell, and others died later, and their memory is maintained by Lionel Rigby's diligent research and writing.

Stoke Poges was no different in its sacrifice from many other Buckinghamshire towns and villages. But today we know more about the lives and families of those who died and of those who survived. The names on the war memorial are now those of real people.

SIR NIGEL MOBBS
HM Lord-Lieutenant of Buckinghamshire

PROLOGUE

Chapter One

The Village before The Great War

John Tarrant,* who died in 1984, recalled the village of his youth in an article he wrote in 1972 entitled 'I Remember'.† He was born in 1898 and started school in 1904. The Council School was in School Lane, having been built in 1876 to serve Stoke Poges and Wexham. A number of the men who served in the war would have attended this local school. John Tarrant, a King's Scout, joined the

1 *The first Stoke Poges scout camp was held at Stoke Place in 1911. George Isbell (assistant scout master) and most of the boys fought in the war and one, John Bateman, who became a boy sailor in 1912, lost his life. Back row, left to right: a visitor, W. Banister (13) (patrol leader), John Clayton (assistant scout master) and Reverend C. Stokes (scout master). Front row, left to right: Albert Edward Isbell (15), John Bateman (14), William Ernest Bateman (12), John Tarrant (13), George Isbell (assistant scout master), Harry Hazell (13), F.Birch, Herbert Taylor (13), Wilfred Ward (15) (patrol leader), Albert Birch (14), A. Andrews (patrol leader), W. Evered, A. Harding.*

The following served in the war: William Banister, 52nd Royal Fusiliers; John Clayton, Army Service Corps; Albert Edward Isbell, Oxford and Bucks Light Infantry; John Bateman, Royal Navy; William Ernest Bateman, Oxford and Bucks Light Infantry; John Tarrant, Coldstream Guards; George Isbell, Essex Regiment; Harry Hazell, Oxford and Bucks Light Infantry; Wilfred Ward, RAF; Albert Birch; A. Andrews, Devon Regiment.

---

* John Tarrant was born in 1898 and educated at Stoke Poges Village School from 1904-12. Appointed a school manager in 1925, he became the school correspondent from 1929-74 when the duties were transferred to the Area Education Officer. He was a scoutmaster in the 1930s and secretary and treasurer of the Village Hall from 1942-51 and then a trustee. He was also treasurer of the Stoke Poges Parochial Church Council. In 1976 his history of the school, *The Village School*, was published to mark the School Centenary.

† 'I Remember', a competition held by the Middle Thames Archaeological and Historical Society in 1972.

Coldstream Guards in April 1917 when he was 18 years old. This is John's description of the school and village prior to the outbreak of the war. What he describes would have been the village way of life familiar to all the men who went away to war.

I Remember Stoke Poges

John Tarrant

The whole school then accommodated pupils up to the age of 14, the boys were in the west wing and the girls in the east wing in separate classes; the infants, up to the age of eight, being all in the centre room. One can still see the indication in large letters on the front of the school – 'Boys' on the left, 'Girls' on the right. The boys had a separate playground and were not allowed to mix with the girls during school hours. Our curriculum was not very extensive and consisted mainly of the three R's; arithmetic and reading each morning and afternoon, history, geography, etc. once a week. Apart from gardening, we had no manual instruction. The top boys' class had practical gardening, each with his own plot, twice a week and the girls had needlework. I suppose the learning we received was just enough to launch us into the world as it existed at that time. There was no question of scholarships for the country lads and lasses and unless our parents could afford to pay for further education it stopped at fourteen. One could, of course, gain further knowledge if we cared to attend evening classes at Slough, usually only in the winter months and then our only means of transport was by cycle if we were lucky enough to possess one.

Transport did not bother us in those days. Beyond Glenister's wagonette which used to run from Stoke Common to the *Reindeer Inn* (long since gone) in the High Street, Slough, twice a week on Wednesdays and Saturdays – down in the morning and back in the afternoon – there was no means of getting to Slough except by private vehicle, cycle or on shank's pony. Mothers used to trundle their prams once a week all the way to Slough and back for shopping. There was a welcome break half way where one could sit on a bench conveniently provided by the side of the road and rest for a while. Traders, of course, came round for orders and delivered goods. We had the baker, the grocer, the butcher, the

2 *The School, School Lane, built 1876. Many of the men who served in the war were pupils at this school.*

3 *The mothers pushing their prams to Slough, referred to by John Tarrant, would have passed St Paul's Church in Stoke Road. It was built in 1906 and Algernon Gilliat was the generous benefactor who financed it. He was a churchwarden at St Giles' Church from 1881 to 1907.*

4 *The senior boys' class of 1910, pupils aged 12, with John Tarrant first on the left, middle row. By 1916 the boys would have been eligible for military service.*

fishmonger, etc. calling regularly but delivered prices were higher and it paid to tramp to Slough for requirements if one could do so. For milk we used to carry the can to Stoke Court dairy after school each day. We would wait beside the door until the dairyman arrived. The milk was contained in huge shallow pans on benches around the dairy and after standing several hours would be ready for the dairyman to take off the cream with a skimmer (cream separators were unknown). The remaining 'skimmed' milk was then retailed to the waiting crowd at 1d. per quart. The milk round was our daily chore.

The village people themselves provided many more of their daily food items than is the case today. All the vegetables and fruit were grown in the back garden, which also housed the chickens – for poultry and eggs – and, on occasion, the pigs, which ate up all the leftovers and were cheap to keep. We had a local part-time pig slaughterer (a bricklayer by trade) who used to go around the cottages and kill the animals as required. Sides of bacon would be salted down; lovely ham and pork joints were provided and the housewife would make use of every part of the pig.

5 *The building known as the 'Cat Farm' as it would have looked in John Tarrant's day. It has since been extended. The original building is early 17th-century and is of red brick, white colour-washed, with some of the original timber framing visible on the front elevation. The old pump with stone bench table, referred to by John Tarrant, is on the left-hand side of the door.*

6 *Gray's Monument. 'Across the church meadows for the morning service'*, c.1905.

7 *Stoke Park Mansion when it was the private residence of Wilberforce Bryant; an early photograph taken in 1892 by H.C.Wilder.*

Very few of the cottages had mains water supply and water had to be drawn at the village pumps or from wells in the back garden. One such pump can still be seen in Bells Hill at the L.H. Engineering establishment then called 'The Cat Farm'.* It was nothing to have to walk several hundred yards with two pails of water perhaps twice or three times a day for the daily requirements. Needless to say water was sparingly used. The bathroom was a tub in front of the kitchen fire on Saturday nights. Water closets were a definite luxury, in most cases unobtainable. A 'privy' at the bottom of the garden was more common and on a cold winter's night: ugh!

For light we had oil lamps and candles. Some estates had their own generators but otherwise electricity was non-existent. Ice pits could be seen on some of the estates, which were filled with natural ice from the ponds, etc. in winter packed so tightly it was still there for use in summertime.

We had some ten or eleven public houses in the village which were open all day and beer was 2d. a pint. One could make merry on very little but then most had very little to make merry on. The daily papers could be had at ½d. per copy. Most of us were content with the weekly at 1d., the reading of which became a Sunday ritual. Sundays were, however, largely occupied by going to church. The villagers streamed across the church meadows for the morning service and others came in their carriages. The church was full to capacity every Sunday morning. Patrons had their own pews allocated and reserved for them but the villagers were accommodated in the 'free' seats behind the choir; the children were seated in the gallery under strict supervision.

Cold frosty mornings in early spring, hazy heat in the long summer days, red gold sunsets in the autumn and snow in the winter were much the same as today although in retrospect it does seem the extremes of climate were more accentuated, probably because the weather impinged more on our comfort. The woods and meadows were extensive and took the place of recreation grounds and playing fields of which we had none. How they abounded with wild life, rabbit, hare, fox, weasel, stoat, red squirrel (since ousted by the grey variety), partridge, pheasant, and much else. In the woods of Stoke Park† a herd of red deer and fallow deer roamed. It was a stirring sight to see the monarch of the forest engaged in mortal combat. (The fights occurred in the mating season when it was dangerous to roam around.) They would go for hours and hours; horn locked against horn until victor and vanquished emerged. Life had its compensations here for many a juicy joint of venison was had from the friendly gamekeeper after a kill. Regular 'shoots' took place in the season and beaters would work through the woods putting up the game for the guns to pick off. It meant a pleasant day's occupation for, possibly, 2s. 6d. with a meal thrown in and probably a rabbit to take home at the end. Very acceptable when work was scarce as was often the case in wintertime.

---

* The 'Cat Farm' was owned by Lady Decies who was well known for her collection of cats and was said to have introduced the Siamese cat to this country. The building was then part of the Sefton Park Estate. Later it was a laundry, it was occupied by L.H.Engineering and is now owned by Chiltern International Ltd.

† At this time Wilberforce Bryant, son of the founder of Bryant and May, owned Stoke Park but he died in 1906. The mansion was empty for two years until sold to Nick 'Pa' Lane Jackson in 1908. He converted the mansion into a country club and Harry Shapland Colt landscaped the 27-hole golf course. By 1914 this provided considerable local employment.

8 *The class of 1908, a generation that missed service in the war, although many would have had brothers in the army or navy.*

9 *Further along Stoke Road is the* BrickmakersArms, *named because of its proximity to the nearby brickfields.*

During the season also Eton College beagles had a regular monthly run chasing hares over the fields and we had the occasional 'Drag Hunt' when the dragman pulled a sack primed with aniseed or some such substance through woods and meadows and hounds and horsemen had a cross-country run following the scent. Woe betide the dragman if he was caught. The opponents of blood sports could hardly have objected to this.

Despite the fame arising from its ancient church and 'country churchyard' the village in those days was really a quiet backwater consisting chiefly of fairly large estates with their retainers. There were the Howard-Vyses at Stoke Place, the Bryants of Stoke Park, Decies at Sefton Park, Allhusens of Stoke Court and Hanburys at Wexham Springs and so forth. At one time we boasted a Lord Mayor of London who resided at Framewood. We were roughly divided into 'landed gentry' and 'villagers', the latter including bailiff, foreman, artisans as well as the gardeners, coachmen and other workers. Labour was cheap; an ordinary gardener had to be content with 18s. per week and such perks as he could get. Many were employed on the estates. Even the parson had nine servants including gardener, errand boy, coachman and stable boy. As there were very few motorcars about (one could go days without a car passing through

10 *William Street, Slough, the Crown Corner, early 20th-century.*

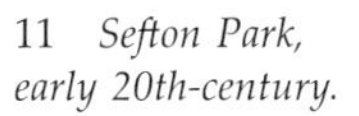
11 *Sefton Park, early 20th-century.*

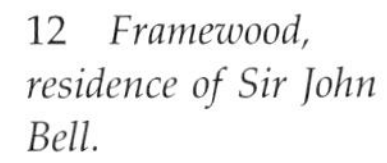
12 *Framewood, residence of Sir John Bell.*

the village) the gentry had their broughams, gigs and 'pony traps'. Carriages with coachman and footmen aboard and a spotted dalmatian trotting at the rear were often to be seen around our lanes and we were expected to doff our caps as my lord and lady rode by. There was no National Insurance or Welfare State and we had to endeavour to remain as healthy as possible. Sickness was an expensive luxury as doctor had to be paid and there was, in the main, no sickness pay to rely on. No unemployment pay either, if one had the misfortune to be out of work. Then families had to rely on their own resources or go 'on the parish' with the workhouse at Slough looming ahead.

We had our village characters. There was Shepherd Edmunds who could be seen with smock, crook and all stomping the road. He lived to be 101 years and 358 days as recorded on his tombstone in the churchyard. There was the innkeeper at the *Rose and Crown* who told all and sundry 'All as goes by 'ere allus come in'. The unfortunate village idiot (we had two) had no mental health organisation to care for him and just had to live with his family until he died.

13 *The church was central to the life of the community. This early photograph shows the extension to the churchyard consecrated in 1911 before the the outer second lychgate was built in 1913.*

14 *Slough Railway Station, familiar to those on the excursions and, later, to the servicemen coming home and returning from leave.*

Many who were without work, and some who did not care to work and had no responsibilities, took to the road. These travellers, tramps or vagrants, were prolific and hardly a day would go by but that one of this fraternity would knock on the cottage door for 'a little tea and sugar missus' or 'a drop of water' for which an old tin can would be proffered. The kindly housewife would often put in a hunk of bread and cheese and mostly these were gratefully accepted. If one cared to look, the traveller could be discovered in a field down the road with a little fire making his tea and enjoying a 'well earned' rest. A doss house was provided at Amersham and another at Slough and the distance between was a convenient day's travel for the tramp. All villages on route had their share of visitations.

We had few distractions and holidays away from home were practically unknown. The Slough Nursing Fund used to run a railway excursion once a year to the seaside and local groups reserved coaches on the train for their annual outing. It was so popular that sometimes three separate trains had to be put on. A different resort was selected each year, places such as Southsea, Brighton and Margate were chosen. Our church choir and bell ringers always had their outing on these excursions, which was something we all looked forward to as one of the events of the year. Up at 5 a.m. after a sleepless night of excited anticipation, at 6.30 a.m. onto a wagon drawn by one or two horses generously provided for the occasion by a local trader, boarding the train at 7 a.m. and, after an exhilarating rail journey of some two to three hours, to the shore for our annual glimpse of the sea. A luscious lunch and tea were provided and after visits to the shops for presents back to the train, tired but happy arriving at, perhaps, 11 p.m. wondering 'where shall we go to next year?'

Trips to London to see relatives, etc. were really special. We had to be early risers to catch the train from Slough at 7 a.m. when we could travel at 'workmen's fares' – 8d return – to Paddington.

Our pleasures were mainly settled on home events of which there were highlights each year. Our chief annual event was the Flower Show at Stoke Place. Always held on the first Wednesday in August. Four large tents of exhibits, Slough Town Band, all the fun of the fair, children's races with dancing on the green in the evening. We prayed for fine weather and usually got it. The local nurseries had a tent to themselves and their displays were truly magnificent. Us school children had two classes only; one for naming wild flowers and one for the best bunches. A local botanist took great interest in these classes and encouraged us to produce fine displays. The vegetables and flowers exhibited by villagers and professionals alike had to be seen to be believed. At times the awards produced disputes as to the merit of the exhibits (and the exhibitors); 'Oi knows 'is garden, 'e never had no marrows like that oi know'. Competition was very keen.

Other annual events were the Parish Tea and the Choir Concert, both held in the winter months. Prior to the building of the Village Hall in 1912 these took place in the Parish Rooms. The Rooms had previously been the Old School and were situated in Rogers Lane.* The building is still there, now made into three houses and the description on the wall shows it as 'The Old School Cottage'. The Junior School is next door.

---

* The school in School Lane closed in 2002 and the Rogers Lane School is now a Combined School.

15 *Burnham Beeches in the early 20th century. Sir Henry Peek, M.P., purchased it in 1879, and resold 374 acres of it to the City of London for use by the public as an open space, particularly by the citizens of London. A further 65 acres was added in 1921, a gift of Viscount Burnham, and additional land was subsequently acquired.*

The Parish Tea cost 6d. a head. A good 'bun fight' was followed by entertainment of music hall proportions. The Choir Concert was eagerly awaited as one of the high spots of the year. Practice started immediately after Xmas and the Concert usually finished the winter season. In addition to these special events whist drives and dances were often arranged and all were well attended; thus we made our own amusements.

Christmas was, as everywhere, eagerly looked forward to. The choir and other 'waits' serenaded our houses; 'While Shepherds' and 'Good King Wenceslas' were the favourites and the gentry kept almost open house with special treats for young and old. The Christmas dinner was always centred on the home. Turkeys were not so plentiful but we had a substitute in good old English roast beef. We liked to see the snow and if it was really cold, skating on lakes and ponds was the order of the day. On one well-remembered occasion we awoke on Boxing morning to find the snow two feet deep. Strenuous efforts were necessary to clear paths and roads. The road to Slough was blocked with ten-foot drifts. What a delight to the boys and girls.

We had a treat in store for the spring and summer bank holidays when families went 'en bloc' to Burnham Beeches. We walked through the lanes and across Brockhurst Wood to Farnham, thence over the Common for a day's enjoyment in the beech woods; sliding down the dells, climbing among the roots and low branches. Or perhaps we had 6d. to spend and there were donkey rides and swings to be savoured; also a shop where trifles could be purchased. Mid-day, out came the sandwiches and bottles of pop for our picnic and, later, we trouped home across woods and fields fully satisfied with our bank holiday. Sometimes, as now, these holidays were wet which meant stay at home with long faces.

Last but not least, mention must be made of the annual visit of the itinerant showmen who, with their roundabouts, swings and side shows, camped on the Common opposite the *Fox and Pheasant* for some three days every July and the village flocked to enjoy 'All the fun of the Fair'.

So the years went on, summer followed winter and there was little change in our mode of life till came a day when the war clouds rolled along the horizon. These passed us by until the fateful day when SARAJEVO was on everyone's lips. We sat up and took notice. On 4 August 1914, we heard the dread news 'War has been declared'. It was the end of an era.

PART ONE

Chapter Two

The Village in the War Years

Prior to the outbreak of the Great War, Stoke Poges had been reduced in area and population by the expansion of Slough pushing the parish boundaries further north. But it still included the area of Slough we now know as Manor Park, at that time farmland.

Stoke Poges consisted of a number of scattered hamlets and settlements. In the south was Stoke Green dominated by Stoke Place, one of the four great houses and estates. The Howard-Vyse family provided employment in the house, gardens and farmlands of their estate.

Stoke Park Mansion, to the west of Stoke Green, had ceased to be a private residence and become a golf course but the estate retained farmland and horticultural interests.

Further to the north Stoke Court was the residence of the Allhusen family and West End, now Rogers Lane, was a small settlement that together with Bells Hill was the centre of the village. Nearby was Sefton Park Estate providing employment at the house and in the gardens and on the farm. Even further north was Stoke Common with its collection of houses in what are now Templewood Lane and the Gerrards Cross Road. Holly Bush Hill led to the Wexham Road side of the parish. Near the school was a small settlement known as Hockley Hole.

This was a rural agricultural parish with Slough its market town. Apart from a small number of craftsmen, employment was in agriculture and domestic service. This was a close-knit community and many of the men who served in the war had attended the local school.

16 *Stoke Place, home of Henry Howard-Vyse and his sons Richard and George. Richard served in the Egyptian Expeditionary Force and George, an invalid, edited the letters from servicemen printed in the Parish Magazine.*

Following the outbreak of war on 4 August 1914, 71 men had volunteered or been recalled from the reserve, nine of them officers. A year later when a notice appeared in a local newspaper suggesting that Stoke Poges contained a great number of 'slackers', the number of those serving had risen to 175 of whom 20 were officers. Since they were mainly volunteers this was a very creditable achievement for a village whose population was only about 1,400. The number listed at the end of the war as having served was 306 including 23 officers and one woman. This total also included men on the War Memorial with a close association with the village such as the two soldiers who married Stoke Poges girls. This was about one in five of the population. At least 45 of them served in the Oxford and Bucks Light Infantry including the Bucks Battalion and nine of them died as a result of the conflict, three in the same battle. Four men became prisoners of war; when men were posted missing, families clung to the hope that they had been taken prisoner.

Stoke Poges men served in all theatres of operations, mostly in Belgium and France of course, but also in Italy, the Dardanelles, Palestine, Mesopotamia, Salonika and one, Major Charles Wakefield, died in what was German East Africa, now known as Tanzania. Sergeant William Lawrence, of the Hampshire

17 *Stoke Park Mansion ceased to be a private residence in 1908 and became a country club and golf course providing much local employment.*

18 *Stoke Court, the residence of Henry Allhusen but used during the war as a hospital for officers of the Royal Flying Corps.*

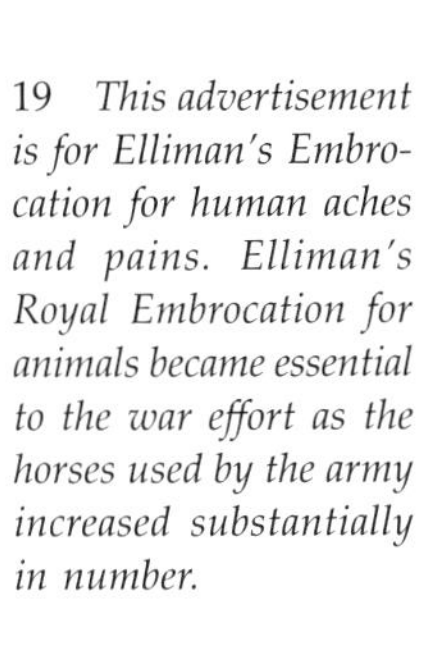

19 *This advertisement is for Elliman's Embrocation for human aches and pains. Elliman's Royal Embrocation for animals became essential to the war effort as the horses used by the army increased substantially in number.*

Regiment, whose brother Alfred died in France, was probably the most travelled. In 1919 the editor of the Parish Magazine wondered if his Christmas parcel would ever reach him since he had written from India, then Singapore, and later a long letter from Hong Kong in which he had given an account of the terrible seas encountered on the China Seas. Finally, he reached Vladivostok.

The Parish Magazine, produced monthly, reached a number of those serving and kept them in touch with each other and with home. The letters from the front, published in the Magazine, are an invaluable record of the experiences of Stoke men. These letters and the service notes were edited and printed each month and involved a great deal of effort in obtaining and returning letters to relatives. The editor until he died in May 1916 was George Howard-Vyse who had been seriously injured in a riding accident. After his death the Magazine continued to publish news and included a list of those serving, updated every month. Short obituaries of those who died were also printed.

Activities were organised in the village in aid of the war effort. A month after the outbreak of war a fund was established to give local relief to supplement the contribution of the Soldiers and Sailors Families' Association and other Societies in relieving distress. Six months later, in March 1915, the fund was criticised because it had spent only £3 11s. in actual relief. In justification of its approach to administering the fund, a member of the committee wrote in the Parish Magazine:

> The Committee, with the valuable assistance of Lady Bisset (the president of the local Soldiers' and Sailors' Families Association), have had to deal with about 20 applications. Instead of giving money – a much easier and more dangerous way – the Secretary (Mr C. Gilliat) has found employment for nearly all the applicants; this has meant spending many hours personally looking into the claims for Relief – and after finding employment – he makes it his business to call round every week and see the employer – and also the employee – and satisfy himself that everything is satisfactory ... The Committee feel confident that all the money subscribed will be required later on, as the pinch has not yet been felt.

Volunteering for the forces could result in hardship for families. One of the local gentry offered £1 to every man enlisting from Stoke during the month of September 1914. This, the Parish Magazine recorded, 'has enabled the soldier to procure for himself some outfit and to leave behind sufficient to tide his family over until pay and allowances become due.' Some 21 men benefited from this gesture.

By the spring of 1915 it was becoming evident nationally that voluntary recruitment would not be sufficient to maintain the numbers required in the army for a long war. A last effort was made in the autumn of 1915 to uphold the voluntary principle through a scheme prepared by Lord Derby, then Director-General of Recruiting. All males between 18 and 45 were asked to enlist or attest their willingness to serve when summoned. By the end of November 1915 nearly half of the eligible single men had not attested, making conscription inevitable the following year. Between 1 March 1916 and 31 May 1917 only 371,000 men were compulsorily enlisted and 779,936 were granted exemption. Locally, the Parish Magazine recorded that 'a good many of our men have put down their names under Lord Derby's scheme'.

It was possible for the self-employed and for employers to appeal to a local tribunal to secure exemption from military service for those in essential employment. In July 1917 Stoke Park Golf Club appealed to secure exemption for Frank Jennings, aged 31, who was a vegetable and fruit grower who worked on ten acres adjoining the grounds of Stoke Park Club. About 80 men had joined up from the staff of the club and seven of them had been killed. Jennings was exempted for six months. A similar application was made for an engineer and electrician at Stoke Park who was the only employee to understand the

20 *Vesta Tilley, the music hall star, used her appearances to further recruitment as illustrated in this photograph. Her husband, Sir Walter de Frece, bought Sefton Park in 1922 and Vesta Tilley lived there for the next six years.*

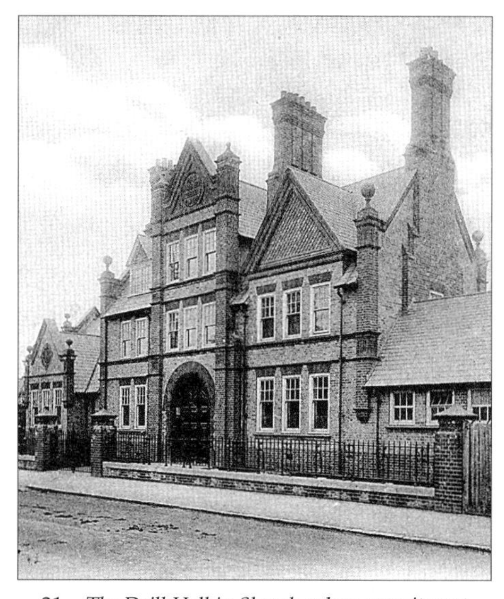

21 *The Drill Hall in Slough, where recruitment took place, was built by James Elliman, then Slough's greatest benefactor.*

22 *Slough High Street showing the Post Office, Town Hall and other buildings.*

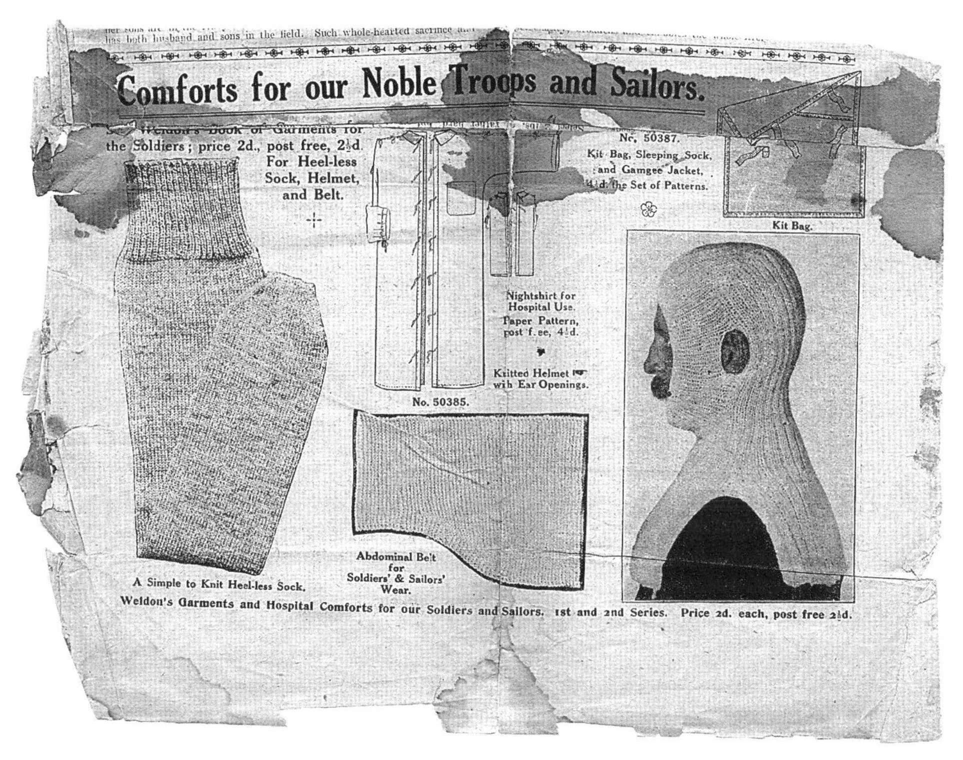

has both husband and sons in the field. Such whole-hearted sacrifice ...

Comforts for our Noble Troops and Sailors.

... Weldon's Book of Garments for the Soldiers; price 2d., post free, 2½d. For Heel-less Sock, Helmet, and Belt.

No. 50387. Kit Bag, Sleeping Sock, and Gamgee Jacket, 4½d. the Set of Patterns.

Kit Bag.

Nightshirt for Hospital Use. Paper Pattern, post free, 4½d.

Knitted Helmet with Ear Openings.

No. 50385.

A Simple to Knit Heel-less Sock.

Abdominal Belt for Soldiers' & Sailors' Wear.

Weldon's Garments and Hospital Comforts for our Soldiers and Sailors. 1st and 2nd Series. Price 2d. each, post free 2½d.

23 *Weldon's Ladies' Journal knitting patterns for garments for servicemen.*

(5)
POST CARD
THIS SPACE MAY NOW BE USED FOR COMMUNICATION
ADDRESS ONLY HERE
Church Army Press, Printers and Publishers, Cowley, Oxford.

The morning each day this week has been beautifully fine & sunny but Sunday and this afternoon have been very wet. On Sat: about 50 Red cross motor cars went by en route for Bristol. They returned on Sunday with wounded 'Tommies'. We have Belgian refugees, and plenty of soldiers at Slough, which is only two miles from Windsor. We can see the Castle from where we are staying.

24 *This message written on a postcard of St Giles' Church sent by a visitor describes the wartime scene in Slough. Out of a million refugees who fled Belgium at the outbreak of war, an estimated 100,000 came to Britain. Stoke House in Stoke Green, formerly Parry's School, provided a home for 50 of these refugees.*

fire appliances and knew where the fire hydrants were located. In August 1917 Mr Allhusen retired from the tribunal to present the appeal for one of his own employees who was a farm estate and gas worker at Stoke Court, then a hospital for officers of the Royal Flying Corps. He was exempted for six months.

The list of men serving, published and updated monthly throughout the war in the Parish Magazine, was paid for by public subscription. In December 1915, 110 parcels were sent to soldiers and sailors who were or had been on active service, and 60 smaller parcels were sent to those on home service. More than £50 was subscribed towards the cost of the parcels together with needlework by some 50 parishioners. Each parcel contained a scarf and a pair of mittens, a pair of socks, two handkerchiefs, a towel, a cake of soap, writing block, pencil and envelopes, cigarettes (or pipe and tobacco), peppermint lozenges (or acid drops), cough lozenges, slab of chocolate, packet of cocoa, sugar and milk tablets, a tin of sardines and a plum pudding. This practice had started the previous year and continued throughout the war. Many letters of thanks were received for these parcels were much appreciated.

The voluntary work in the parish to further the war effort covered a great variety of activities. Knitting socks was an all year round task in order to produce sufficient pairs for the Christmas parcels. A campaign to produce fresh vegetables for the fleet resulted in many cases being transported each Friday to Slough Station. The School had a 20-pole plot cultivated by 20 boys to grow vegetables for the fleet. In 1917 children at the School made excursions to pick blackberries for jam. They collected 800 lbs and were told they had done something for the health of the soldiers and sailors because blackberry jam had a certain medicinal value. Horse chestnuts were also collected for munitions to replace barley. One ton of horse chestnuts replaced half a ton of barley. Three tons were collected in the autumn of 1917. Money was also collected for a variety of good causes and raised by holding concerts in the newly built village hall.

As Driver Isbell wrote in a letter home, 'Everyone in Stoke is doing their share, even the school-children.' Life had changed during the war years with so many men away. There was hardship and anxiety for loved ones, yet there was commitment to the war effort and the men in the forces were kept in touch with what was happening in their village.

Chapter Three

Letters from The Front

There is a great deal of information in the Parish Magazines from late 1914 until 1919 about the men who left Stoke Poges to serve in the war. A selection of letters, and extracts from letters, recount their experiences and how they faced up to the challenges they were presented with in the conditions in which they found themselves, sometimes many hundreds of miles from home.

Letters written by men who died have been included in their obituaries. One, in particular, Walter Gutteridge, was a prolific letter writer with a fine eye for descriptive narrative.

Some of the names of roads in Stoke Poges where men lived have changed. For example, Farnham Road is now Templewood Lane and Uxbridge Road is now Hollybush Hill.

The First Battle of Ypres

Private Edward Elderfield, 2nd Battalion, Oxford and Bucks Light Infantry, Wexham Street, December 1914 Parish Magazine.

In one of the first letters from the front Ted Elderfield describes the action on 11 November 1914 when a Prussian Guards Division attempted to break through the British lines just north of the Menin Road. They were halted and then cleared from the Nonne Bosschen (Nun's Wood) by a determined counter-attack by the 2nd Battalion of the Oxford and Bucks.

25 *Ted Elderfield.*

> … A few lines to let you know I am all right and having a bit of a blow after some very rough times – and lucky I am to be alive, as they have been coming up very thick and going back very thin. I have seen some sights I shall never forget – dead Germans in hundreds. They broke through the other day, and we had to go and round them up. We drove them through a wood and then charged the trenches, and you should have seen them run and hold up their hands! And they were big fellows too – German Guards. We took the trenches, and it did thunder and lightning at night. I had to go and carry wounded in, and carried one officer about three miles. He took our names and addresses, and said he would send us something when he got to England. We are having some rough weather; it snowed all day yesterday – the ground is covered – and frost at night. I am in a loft now with a blanket round me, but I expect it won't be long before I am up again … I can't write any more as I have got to go on parade. I don't know what it is. Goodbye.

Life in the Trenches

Private Alexander MacLean, 2nd Battalion, Grenadier Guards, Stoke Park.

The first account of life in the trenches, published in the Parish Magazine in February 1915, came from Private Alexander MacLean of the Grenadier Guards who lived in Stoke Park. At the end of the war he was a corporal. In a letter dated 5 January 1915, he wrote:

> We have been in the trenches at the firing line, and the times we have been relieved do not give one an opportunity of writing. The time is fully occupied by drying – clothes, restoring and getting together kit, &c. The weather has been wet and the soil here is clay, so we come out like masses of mud.
>
> We had a very sharp engagement with the Germans all Christmas Eve,* beginning in the morning. Our Company† suffered severely. The Captain, Sir Montague Cholmeley, and a Lieutenant being killed and another officer wounded, besides a considerable number of NCOs and men. The Germans attacked with a new device – a kind of bomb or grenade, which they throw from a gun from their trenches, high in the air. It explodes, when it comes down, with a greater explosion than a shell and sends splinters all over the place. The advantage, however, is that we can easily see it coming and soon learned to identify the report of its particular gun; so we merely watch it, and, if it threatens to come into the trench, 'shoot off' round the corner and keep low. On Thursday morning the British artillery got the range beautifully and made splendid practice at them with shrapnel; the shells passing over our heads, bursting from fifty to a hundred yards in front of us, and sweeping their trenches.
>
> They renewed the attack again at night and kept us with fixed bayonets all night, but did not do anything in the way of charging. The artillery again came to our support and in the morning their attack 'fizzled out' and left our line intact. The amount of ammunition they use is enormous. They shoot lighted 'candles' over our positions all night long and, as these come down, they light up all the scene. By far their most deadly game, though, is sniping. Firing through a loophole, for instance, is very dangerous unless the loophole is made very carefully

---

* The 2nd Battalion had taken over the line at Rue de Cailloux near Le Touret after dark on 23 December 1914. These were new trenches and were very bad having been hastily improvised from dykes after the Germans had captured the front-line trenches. The War Diary describes the fighting referred to by Alexander MacLean. 'The early morning began with considerable sniping and bombardment with trench mortars … The enemy had the advantage of the ground, for not only did his trenches drain into ours, but he was able to overlook our whole line. In addition to this he was amply supplied with trench mortars and hand grenades, so that we were fighting under very great difficulties. He mined within ten yards of our trench, after which he attacked in great force, but was unable to more than just reach our line.' The diary then records that Captain Sir Montague Cholmeley, Bart., and Second Lieutenant J.H. Neville had been killed and Second Lieutenant G.G. Goschen wounded and taken prisoner. Lieut. Goschen had only escaped drowning in the trench because one of his men had propped him up in time.

† The structure of the army, together with the ranks of the commanders of the various units, was broadly: Infantry Section, NCO, 10 men; Platoon, 2nd Lt, 50 men; Company, Capt (2i/c Lt), 220 men; Battalion, Lt Col (2i/c Maj.), 1,000 men; Brigade, Brig Gen, 5,000 men; Division, Maj.Gen, 15,000 men; Corps, Lt Gen, 36,000 men; Army, Gen, 180,000 men.

concealed. But one soon realises when he is being sniped, and as they are very persistent the best thing to do is to shift position.

The worst part of the trench fighting is the getting to and from the firing line. There is a long communication trench first to traverse and one often has to wade knee-deep or even waist-deep in water, or, what is worse, through the clay soil where you sink and stick. Rifles also catch the mud and it gets into the bolt and magazine and makes firing difficult. We were relieved yesterday and this Battalion shifted to billets four miles back for, I think, a few days' rest, although we have continually to have all our equipment and ammunition ready to move at a moment's notice.

Our Company is reduced a lot, including over a dozen cases of frost-bite in the feet the day after Christmas. It was very cold then. We are supplied with skin coats and the people of England have been very kind in sending out woollen things; scarves, gloves, &c., which are much appreciated. The parcel came most opportunely as I had lost or used all my spare kit this last fortnight. New Year's Day passed without anything great going on, except that me and a mate in the same trench were being sniped all day, owing to an unfortunate loophole we made the previous night. I think part of a sandbag showed up against some black earth. There was a good deal of artillery firing but they did no damage. About midnight the Germans gave us a tremendous fusillade of rifle-fire. It began far on our right and came on like a gigantic 'Feu-de-Joie'. For about fifteen minutes the bullets came like a hailstorm – and then it died away.

I think they are taking in the New Year, but am not sure. Anyway we did not take any notice of it. Afterwards we could hear them playing mouth-organs and see the glimmer of fires in their trenches. We, of course, fire at this. The countryside round here is flat and low lying, and for a number of miles back is dotted with graves giving the names of the Regiments the men belonged to, who are buried. Villages are all destroyed, or partly so, particularly large buildings such as churches, &c., which are supposed to have been used as observation stations, and, generally the country is desolate. Men are few and no work is done, and all the women wear black clothes. I think I will now close as the candle I write by (in a barn about half a dozen miles from the firing line) is getting short, and they want the lights out here very early. I trust you are well in Stoke Poges. Again, thanking you all for the gifts

Yours sincerely,
A.J. MacLean

P.S.- I forgot to say that the German firing on Christmas morning died away and altogether ceased, and just afterwards we had an order passed down to us for nobody to fire without orders; so we had peace for Christmas forenoon. And an officer came up to the trenches to say that the Prince of Wales, who was somewhere just in the rear, wished us all a happy Christmas.

Trench Life – Another View

A Stoke Poges Soldier, May 1915:

> Yesterday we got up to the high place of the roof of a house, whence we got a good view of both lines of trenches – both ours and the Germans. It was rather extraordinary to see the smoke of the cooking fires of both lots along a front of perhaps four miles.
>
> It all looked so peaceful in the sun that it was hard to believe that any man who tried to look over the parapet of his trench would be instantly killed almost for certain.

The routine was spells in and out of the trenches and being a witness to death and the effect of losses on a battalion or company. The next letter from Pte E. Elderfield described his feelings and what he witnessed.

In and Out of the Trenches

Private Edward Elderfield, 2nd Battalion, Oxford and Bucks Light Infantry, Wexham Street, May 1915:

> I shall never forget our old Regiment (Oxford and Bucks Light Infantry) marching into the town of B-. There were only four hundred, and I think we have been reinforced seven times then. And we came here over a thousand strong. So we had lost a few! And what were left of us were knocked up. They tried to whistle – but it soon died down. But after a week's rest you should have seen them. They could buy a pork chop and a few luxuries, so they did themselves a bit of good, and you could soon see the difference.
>
> We have got a fine lot of men out here now, and a good few have got the South Africa ribbon up.
>
> We have a few casualties – always leaving one or two behind in the burial ground. We have got some pretty graveyards behind the firing line with a cross and the name, regiment and date; flowers are planted on them and they look nice. The other day I saw a most touching sight. One of our men had been shot through the head. The Coy Sergt Major read the Service and the other men stood round bare-headed. I thought it a fine tribute to a man who had fallen for the Country's sake.
>
> Of course there are times when this is impossible; but, whenever we can, we pay due respect by placing a cross on the grave and turfing it. As you will know by now, I am a stretcher-bearer. I have been at work since Christmas as we lost most of our stretcher-bearers at Ypres. When we are in reserve we have lectures on first aid by the doctors.

An Army Service Corps View

Driver John Clayton, Army Service Corps, Bells Hill, June 1915.
Letter dated 8 May 1915:

> I have been out here now six weeks, and during that time we have travelled a great deal in France. We had our convoy shelled on the sixth day we were out here, but we managed to get through with the food for

the boys in the trenches. It was our 'Baptism of Fire'. Up to the present time I have not seen anything of the other Stoke Poges boys who are out here, but may do so as the regiments come down to the rest camps. Our artillery are just starting again to let old 'Bill's' blokes know that we are not asleep, and the report of the guns nearly shakes our old barn down. We are on all day, as hard as we can go, from daylight to dark, so that we don't have to keep the boys in the trenches waiting for their food.

When the Canadians, who fought so bravely at Ypres, came back to their rest camp, they passed by where we are staying, and they had lost everything except their rifles and bandoliers, and the poor fellows could hardly crawl along.

Have been into Belgium, and the towns and villages are one mass of tottering ruins, with holes in the streets – caused by 'Jack Johnsons'* – big enough to bury a wagon in. Most of the people have left, but a few remain, living in the houses that are not quite so badly damaged.

It is a good thing to think our country is not over-run by an invader and devastated as Belgium is. If only the slackers in England could see what we have seen perhaps they would pluck up courage and join the Army to help crush those who have laid Belgium waste.

A Flanders Diary

A Stoke Poges Soldier, June 1915:

April 28th. We are all living in the basement of a house. We had to walk up here, five miles, leaving our horses behind us. Even so, they were shelled yesterday and we lost 20 – including one of mine. There must have been a tremendous expenditure of ammunition – the gunfire never stopped from the evening of 23rd till the morning of 27th. Since then it has slackened off a little – except for every now and then. The 'bulge' in the line has made Ypres more awkward to hold than ever.

There is a garden opposite here – quite ruined of course – but there is a patch of lilies of the valley that will be out in about a week.

May 1st We are still living in the basement. By day – except every now and then – you can walk about quite safely, but at night the Germans shell all the roads and the country between them very heavily, in order to catch reinforcements and supplies coming up. They keep at it all night more or less – but it doesn't keep me awake. By jove it would be nice to get home to see the lilacs – even this beastly Flanders is looking quite pretty.

In the middle of the bombardment last night the Col. of the ------th heard a nightingale in a wood – just behind his trenches – which was being shelled at the moment. The birds don't seem to care a bit.

May 2nd We left our basement this evening. I came away early, but, just as the General left with B., they saw this infernal gas starting again – great, thick, green, clouds of it – 150 feet high. They had got three or

* 15-cm exploding shells with black smoke and a deep roar named after Jack Johnson, the black American world heavyweight boxing champion, also called 'Black Marias'.

four miles away, but felt – and do still – as if they had very bad colds on their chests. The swines tried the same game on Hill 60 yesterday, but after a bit the wind changed and blew it all back again into the Germans.

Such an invention of the Devil will surely bring its own reward, but, until we find an antidote for it, it is a very serious matter indeed, when the conditions favour its use by the Germans. Apparently they have no real antidote for it themselves, as they do not advance behind it for some time.

May 7th The Germans are lying about their advance east of Ypres, as the British retired long ago as far as they intended to, and did not lose in doing so. We have got a little bit of Hill 60 back and have repulsed two small German attacks elsewhere, with heavy loss to them.

May 12th The French are very pleased with their attack. They have got 47 officers, 2,982 men, 11 guns and 32 machine-guns – and they have got a nice few more shut up in a place with only one 'bolt hole', where they are pretty sure to 'nobble' them.

At Ypres the Germans keep shelling our trenches, and trying to get their infantry to attack! They have dressed some of them in khaki and kilts, but this does not seem to encourage them much! When they attack they usually do so in masses. Nearly all their attacks have been repulsed quite easily, and in one case when they got into our trenches we took them back without difficulty. This is very significant, I think, and very tantalising, too, for it shows if only we could get past their machine guns and other contrivances we should 'get a move on them'.

Great excitement here yesterday as six cygnets were hatched out! Last night there were quite six nightingales within 200 yards of our house. I have found a robin's nest with six eggs and a yellow hammer's with three. We have got masks now, which are all right against the poisonous gas.

A Wounded Man Writes from his Hospital Bed

A Wounded Stoke Soldier, August 1915:

For the time I was in Flanders our battalion was in the 14th Light Infantry Brigade, and the 5th Division, and was in action in different parts of the line from Neuve Eglise to Hill 60. We were kept very busy the whole of the time except for about four days before Whitsun.

At daybreak on Whit-Monday we attempted to carry an attack, the main force being aimed at Hill 60. A whole Cavalry brigade came up to help carry the advance, but they were 'spotted' by the Germans and we were then gassed – the wind being in the German's favour. The Cavalry were obliged to retire and the whole line of Infantry had to hang on at that point as best they could. We being on the right flank did not get such a great amount of gas as the others did, but it was bad enough; luckily our respirators and helmets served their purpose well. We had two men put out of action by the gas; and one has since died of gas poisoning, but we had a considerable number of wounded. So much for our Whitsun Bank Holiday.

26 *The Cloth Hall at Ypres showing the damage caused by German artillery fire in October and November 1914. IWM photograph.*

From then right until I was wounded they tormented us badly; and shelled Ypres continually, finally bringing down the Church, which stood next to the Cathedral.*

We completed a new trench in front of our old fire-trench and 70 yards from theirs and they sapped out and built a small fire-trench 150 yards long, midway between them and us and, in spite of our worrying them continually day and night with mortars and bombs, they managed to fortify it and rained bombs etc. into our trench. Being only 35 yards off, we suffered badly but returned all the attacks. But the pluck and ambition of both sides proved equal.

Then procuring a Battery (Royal Garrison Artillery), we had it mounted in our trench, and, at daybreak on June 1st, opened fire at 35 yards point-blank range, bombarding their trench.

The first shell gave a very fine display of sandbags flying in all directions, and of surprised Germans trying to escape over the back-ground, but rifle and machine-gun fire soon put a stop to that. After the last shell had been fired their trenches looked very dilapidated, and we thought we really had put a check on their handiwork there. But, no; undaunted they dug it out again the following night, although we absolutely rained bullets into them while they were at it. So then an attack was planned; two mines were placed under their trench, and it was blown up and captured the day after I was wounded, so, worse luck, I was not there to see it.

It was during their continual bombardment of our trench that one of their shells (the kind we call 'Whizz-Bangs')† dropped about ten feet over the parapet of the traverse I was in. The whole side of the trench gave way and fell in on me, and it was half-an-hour before I could be freed, my legs and the lower part of my body getting the worst of it.

---

* The writer is referring to the Gothic Cloth Hall at Ypres destroyed by German artillery.
† 77-millimetre field-gun shell.

I carried on for several days, not wishing to report sick unless it was absolutely necessary.

A few days later, when we came out of the fire trenches into reserve, the Germans started shelling our supports coming up and we took refuge in the reserve bivouacs: but, as the shelling ceased for a little while, several of us – including myself – being warned for guard, came out of the dug-out. A shell came straight overhead, taking off the top of the tree I was standing by, and I was bowled over like a rabbit and could not move. My chum came and dragged me into the bivouac and found I was hit in the neck under the right ear.

When I reached the hospital I was operated on and the shrapnel was found lodging behind my windpipe – it was a rough piece of brass, about as long as a bullet only thinner and wedge shaped.

I am glad to say my wound is now better.

A Stretcher Bearer's View of the Trenches

Private Edward Elderfield, 2nd Battalion, Oxford and Bucks Light Infantry, Wexham Street, September 1915.*

Letter dated 27 July 1915:

All the boys are keeping well. We have just come out of the trenches for our usual turn in reserve. We had a very good time in our last trenches, although we lost one poor fellow killed and three others wounded. It was rather hot with *Whizz-Bangs*, as we call them. They are a little field gun I should think, and you cannot hear them till they burst, but they don't do a lot of damage. Then comes the *German sausage* from the trench mortar, it is shaped like a tip-cat and you can see it coming, and it makes a row like a *Jack Johnson*.

They are some good trenches these, one can get lost as easy as you like, no one would believe what it is like unless they had seen them. We are quite two miles back when we come out into the open. We are making some good dugouts in them.

We had three mines exploded near us but I don't know the results; they are marvellous, I think, our Engineers.

I am wondering what way they can find to fight next; they are over – and underground, on and under the sea and also in the air. I don't see that they can find any other way, do you?

I have just heard from my old chum W. Gutteridge and he has joined up again. He said he had had a fine time and I am pleased his foot is better. They all say he looks very well.

We have just got a new kind of stretcher and I had to leave this letter to go and see the working of it. It is very hard to carry a wounded man on a long stretcher down these trenches as they are not straight, and we have a job to get round the traverses: so we have got this short stretcher instead and I think it will work all right. A man will be more sitting with a strap to support his back.

---

* The 2nd Battalion formed part of the 5th Brigade, 2nd Division, throughout the War.

I have seen my brother Alfred, he is quite close and is a Sergeant in the ASC, attached to the 28th Field Ambulance, and I am going to see him again to night.

Dick Thompson, Lance Corporal Mitchell and I went to a concert given by the 2nd Division* last night. It was very good, but I think – although I am blowing my own trumpet – that our own Regiment provided the best turn. We have got a comic chap, who is very good and dresses up for it well. It was his living in civilian life.

I hope the 'slackers' are stamped out and that all Stoke Poges people are doing their bit, in this great fight for England, Home and Glory.

Supplying the Front Line

Private Victor Reuben Burgess, Motor Transport, Army Service Corps, Bells Hill, September 1915.

Letter dated 8 August 1915:

We get some excitement now and again watching aeroplanes being shelled. There was a lot of fighting going on last night. They started at 6.30 and got going until 11.30; then there was a lull until 3 a.m. when they started again. I was on guard and could see the shells bursting. They lit the sky up just like lightning.

We have to run up the lines at night with no lamps on the lorries and each one is 400 yards apart, so it takes a bit of doing to follow: but one gets used to it in time. I have not come across any Stoke chaps yet, but I guess I shall some day.

The French people here are very kind to us and make us welcome in their houses. A lot of them are refugees and they tell some terrible tales about the way the Germans treated them – how they made old men walk in front of them to be shot down and various other crimes. They have had a terrible time.

Resting after Trench Duty

Private Richard Thompson, 2nd Battalion, Oxford and Bucks Light Infantry, Sefton Cottages, September 1915.

Letter dated 9 August 1915:

Everything seems pretty quiet in the trenches – bar so much bomb-throwing – rifle grenades and so on. I don't mean hand grenades. The last twice in the firing line I have been placed in an advance sap for the purpose of throwing bombs in case the Germans should attack us, but I have never even had to open the box – so you can tell it was pretty quiet as regards them coming towards us.

We are now having our usual eight days rest, and I have been doing a bit of harvesting this morning for a French farmer, putting the corn into stooks for him. They do their harvesting quite differently to us; but I'll write again shortly and tell you how I get on with it. Private Elderfield and Lance Corporal Mitchell are well.

An Air Duel – October 1915

Gunner William Gutteridge, 128th Battery, Royal Field Artillery, Farnham Road, November 1915.

Letter dated 5 October 1915:

27 *William Gutteridge.*

> I witnessed a thrilling duel in the air the other day, between one of our airmen and a German. The German came over our lines, being constantly shelled by our anti-aircraft guns, which made him shiver when, all at once, one of our airmen came out of the clouds, right in front of him, and then the battle began. Our fellow had him whacked right from the start, for he got his machine-gun on him straight away. The German tried hard to get back to his own lines, but his machine must have been riddled with bullets for he dropped like a stone from a height of 2,000 feet. The charred bodies of the occupants of the German machine were picked up and decently buried. Our airman circled over once to make sure he knew the place and then went off to make his report.
>
> We gave him a good cheer, but I don't expect he heard us for the noise of his engine.

An Assault on the Trenches – Saving an Officer

Private George Davis, 2nd Battalion, Oxford and Bucks Light Infantry, Rogers Lane, November 1915.

George Davis in his letter describes fighting during the Battle of Loos, 25 September to 14 October 1915. Two battalions of the Oxfordshire and Buckinghamshire Light Infantry, the 2nd and the 5th, took part in subsidiary attacks to assist the main attack. Two Stoke Poges men died in this battle. In an action by the 5th Battalion on 25 September to take Bellewaarde Farm in the Ypres Sector, Harry Hammond was wounded and later died of his wounds.

George Davis was one of the men of the 2nd Battalion in the trenches near Givenchy and involved in heavy fighting on 25 September. Relieved on 28 September, they reached billets at Essors on 29 September. On 1 October they marched from Essors to Vermelles (eight miles) then marched up the Hulluch road, past old British first-line trenches, into the old German first-line and on to a gun trench (three miles). This was a line of German gun emplacements with several guns having been left behind.

For the next few days there was little activity but heavy shelling. On 4 October they were relieved and returned to billets at Beuvry. It was from Beuvry that George wrote his letter.

Ralph Stahr died at the end of the battle, on 13 October, at Hulluch, fighting with the Gloucestershire Regiment. He was the second Stoke Poges man to lose his life.

Letter dated 8 October 1915:

> When I reported to the Entrenching Battalion I found that all my comrades had rejoined the regiment, so, of course, I was not long in following them.

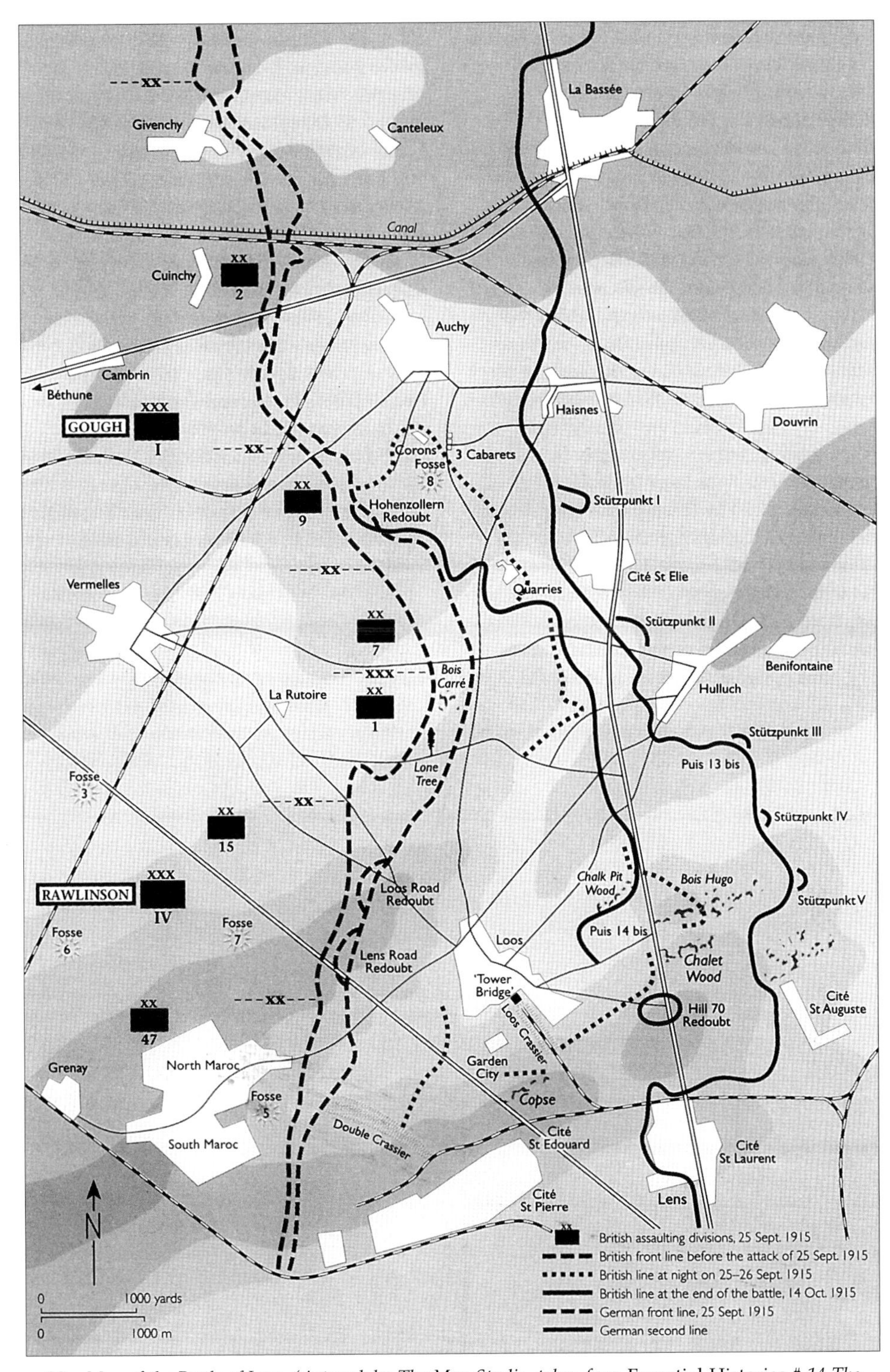

28 *Map of the Battle of Loos. (Artwork by The Map Studio, taken from* Essential Histories # 14 *The First World War, The Western Front 1914-16, written by Peter Simkins, © Osprey Publishing Ltd.)*

29 *2nd Battalion Oxford and Bucks in Beuvry.*

Since then we have been in some very warm corners but I am pleased to say we – the Stoke Boys – are well.

During the assault at ------ my platoon officer fell wounded and I had orders to take charge of him. I dragged him as best I could to a dugout, where I dressed his wounds. In the meantime the Germans were pouring shells of all calibres into us, making the dugout, where we were, very unsafe. So when it got too hot, I thought I would try and remove him to a safer place. I hunted around and found a stretcher-bearer and, between us, we managed to remove him about 150 yards further back into another dugout.

Then I returned to get some field dressings I had left behind, but, when I got there, the whole thing was blown in, so, you see, I only got him away just in time.

I met Ted Elderfield in one of the trenches just afterwards and, as usual, he was working like a nigger (the stretcher-bearers are kept very busy in a job like that). He told me Dick Thompson was all right, so we felt quite relieved to think our boys were safe. Lance Corporal Mitchell was in reserve that day.

The last place we were in the trenches we were able to see for ourselves the extent of the British advance there. You can judge for yourselves that it was considerable; as we had to march about two miles further to take up our position in the front line trenches.

The worst part of that position was that we had to go about three miles to get water, and all the way were exposed to the enemy's fire. One day I volunteered with some others to go and fetch water and, as we were on our way back, they spotted us and gave us a pretty warm time with shrapnel, but luckily no one was hit.

We are at present resting, and have been out now for five days. I cannot say when we shall be going in again.

Life in the Trenches and Mining Activity

A Stoke Poges Soldier, Bucks Battalion, November 1915.

An old pupil of Mr Batten, the headmaster of the local school, writing from France, where he was serving in the Bucks Battalion, describes life in the trenches:

I am writing this just behind the firing line, where we are having a short rest after a strenuous time in the trenches.

We had three months in the trenches in Belgium, and some very exciting times, as we were only a hundred yards from the German lines. But we had a good advantage over them, there being a large wood behind our lines which gave good cover for our artillery, who gave the Germans a very rough time, and behind their lines it was open country, so that they could not get their guns close enough to shell our trenches.

They used to send plenty of rifle grenades over, which are nearly as bad as shells, and they would often call to us in English.

Our engineers exploded a sap under their trench and blew up about thirty yards of it. The enemy also had been mining and exploded a mine a few days later; but it only reached our barbed wire, so did not do any damage at all. When one of these mines explodes it makes the ground shake for miles around.

We are about 600 yards behind the trenches here, so we got plenty of shells and shrapnel.

Percy Plumridge is quite well; he and I often have the old school songs and poetry over in the trenches.

Sergeant W. Pargeter's Dugout

Sergeant William Pargeter, 1st Battalion, Royal Scots, Stoke Common, December 1915.

The previous April he had been slightly wounded in the head when a grenade burst in the trench amongst seven of them. It killed three and wounded three but he was lucky as they were all sitting close to each other.

Letter dated 13 October 1915:

We have moved since I last wrote to you, and are now (Oct.13th) well on the right of the line. There is not much fighting going on where we are at present except with bombs, grenades, and mining. The trenches are not so good as our last ones, and the communication-trench is about three miles long and very narrow, which makes it hard work getting in and out.

I have a very comfortable little dugout, with a bed and table and a fireplace: some of the dugouts are twelve feet below the surface, so are fairly safe.

I have the Magazine every month, and I am glad to see the lads are going on well. I have not had the pleasure of meeting any of them out here yet.

The trenches are swarming with rats, and we pass the time at night killing them. It is very good sport, too, and we are allowed to keep dogs for that purpose.*

* The Battalion War Diary for 4 October 1915 reads: 'Battalion marched to Cappy to new trenches relieving the Royal Irish Regiment. These trenches had recently been taken over from the French and required much hard work to put them into a satisfactory order.' On 12 October, the day before the letter was written, they had relieved the 2nd Camerons in the same trenches. Cappy is 15 miles from Amiens.

A Prisoner of War in Gottingen, Hanover

Private S. Hagger, 4th Battalion, Royal Fusiliers, Farnham Road, December 1915:

> I hope you got the harvest up in fine weather, and that it was a good one. I am very glad to hear that the lads from the village who are at the front are well. I expect they are a bit busy now (October 1st).
>
> I don't suppose there will be much hunting this year. I expect all sport is at a standstill, but it will be much better sport when it begins in earnest in the brighter time to come, which I hope will not be long. But it seems a long time to us.
>
> I don't think there is anything we want – only eatables, that is the only trouble at present.

A Dangerous Mission

A Stoke Poges Soldier, January 1916:

> We have had a good rest, but we are going into the trenches again on Sunday, and it is above our knees in water and mud, so it won't be very comfortable; but if the Huns can stick it I am sure we English can.
>
> The last time we went into the trenches I had rather a dirty bit of work to do. This was to get out on the top of the trench and run about 50 yards in the open across to the Coldstream Guards' trench with a tape, dragging the tape so that we should know where to dig a trench across to them. Every ten yards I had to fall down out of the way of the lights from the Germans.
>
> I never want another job like that. I never stopped to jump into the Coldstreams' trench with the tape, but just fell in head first. I thought my time was come, and I think I am lucky to be alive for I was the fifth man to be sent across. The other four went under, poor chaps.

The Gallipoli Peninsula

Private J.A. Butler, 7th Battalion, Gloucestershire Regiment, Bells Hill, October 1915.

The Allied landings at Gallipoli commenced 25 April 1915 and the campaign ended with the evacuation during the night of 8/9 January 1916. Two Stoke Poges brothers, Bertie and Ernest Butler,* fought there, both serving in the 7th Battalion,† Gloucestershire Regiment. In a letter to his wife, Private J.A. (Bertie) Butler, writes about his Gallipoli experiences:

30 *Bert Butler.*

> Just a line to let you know I have been wounded in the right arm between the elbow and the shoulder with a

* Five Butler brothers served in the war, Ernest and Bertie (J.A.) in the Gloucestershire Regiment, Richard in the Royal Fusiliers, Oscar in the Bucks Territorials and Fred in the Durham Light Infantry. Bertie was taken prisoner 23 March 1918.

† The 7th Battalion arrived at Mudros on the Aegean island of Lemnos, the base for the Gallipoli operation, and a week later sailed for Gallipoli, landing on 'Y' Beach on 11 July 1915. They were relieved and embarked for Mudros arriving 29 July 1915. They returned to Anzac Cove on 3 August 1915.

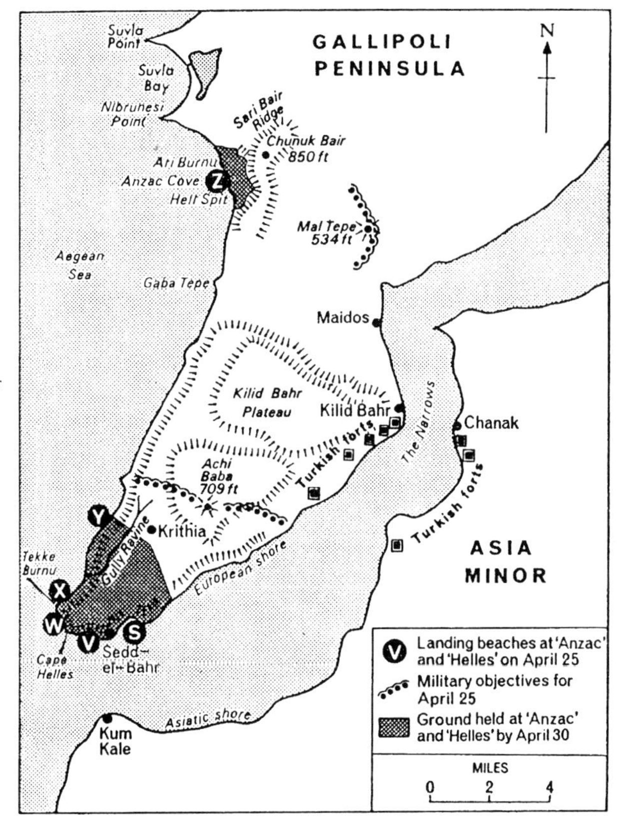

31 *Map of Gallipoli Peninsula reproduced by kind permission of Sir Martin Gilbert, CBE., D.Litt.*

shrapnel bullet, but I have got the bullet and shall bring it home with me when I come; but I don't know when that will be, I'm sure. Don't worry about me, for I am getting on lovely, or I shouldn't be able to write to you.

I got hit when we were in a charge. It is awful out here – no one knows except those who have been in it, and you can't explain it. I can consider myself very, very lucky, I can assure you.

They do look after you so well in the hospital, it's simply wonderful; nothing seems too hard for them to do for you, and it seems a treat to get somewhere for a rest and out of the noise of the shells and bullets whizzing over your heads.

I got wounded on Sunday morning, 8th of August, about 12 o'clock.*

According to the way the Australasians are sticking to it I don't think it can last very much longer. If you look in the newspaper you will see very near where it was, and we were in the thick of it.

* William Ewing, a Chaplain serving on Gallipoli, noted in his book *From Gallipoli to Baghdad* ... 'In the early morning of the 8th, the crest of Chunuk Bair was captured. A unique and glorious record is that of the 7th Gloucesters, a regiment of the New Army. Every officer and senior NCO was either killed or wounded. Reduced to a few small groups of men, commanded by junior NCOs and privates, they fought dauntlessly from midday until sunset.' War Diary records survivors taking three days to rejoin the battalion at Overton Gully. Casualties – three officers killed, eight wounded. Other ranks recorded as approximately 45 killed, 115 wounded, 190 missing.' Westlake, Ray, *British Regiments at Gallipoli* (1996), pp.110/111.

32 *Landing troops and horses at the Dardanelles.*

> I hope you are keeping all right and the children. I should like to see the little dears. I expect they wonder where I am.
>
> It is still very hot out here, and the flies are a torment. There are lots of things I should like to tell you, but I can't.

Private Ernest Butler, 7th Battalion, Gloucestershire Regiment, Uxbridge Road, January 1916.*

Ernest Butler, like his brother, survived Gallipoli although later, in 1917, he was wounded and he lost an arm. His wife received this letter from Malta where he was in hospital:

> Just a few lines to tell you that I am progressing as well as can be expected. I am in the hospital at Malta with frostbitten feet and rheumatism. Well we did have it rough on the 26th of November.† I shall never forget it as long as I live. We had just laid down when the rain and thunder and lightning came on, and it was 2ft. deep in less than an hour. By the time it had finished our trenches were full of water up to the top, 6ft. or more, and then the sides collapsed. How I got out God only knows. A lot of poor fellows got drowned. The Turks were worse off than us. After the monsoon was over we had to dig ourselves in before daylight. Fancy digging wet through to the waist, and we had to stay there for the rest of the day, not allowed to move, or we should have been shot. Well, they soon started shelling us. Then we had orders to go to the firing line that was full of mud and water; and then that night it started snowing and freezing, and the wind was awful – it blew you off your feet. I was blown over several times myself, and poor chaps were lying frozen to death everywhere, and you couldn't help them; it was enough to look after yourself. There were only 15 left of our battalion on the Peninsula.

---

* 'NOVEMBER War Diary notes (26th) much of Battalion's property and equipment destroyed in flood, almost all records lost. Heavily shelled (29th) – 6 killed, 15 wounded. One man died of exposure. Two men died of exposure (30th).' Westlake, Ray, *British Regiments at Gallipoli* (1996), p.111. The Battalion left Gallipoli on 8 January 1916 via 'W' Beach, sailed to Mudros.

† The reference to 26 November is to a well-documented bout of foul weather that added urgency to the need for politicians in London to accept the military advice and confirm the evacuation of the Gallipoli Peninsula – see James, Robert Rhodes, *Gallipoli*, pp.334/336.

First Hand Experience

A Stoke Poges Soldier, February 1916:

The weather continues very dull and rainy. I have read in a paper that 'wet trenches hardly exist out here this winter', and, if I had my own way, I would like to dump the person that wrote it in any one of the trenches here and give him the same experience of mud and water that we are having.

The Ambulance Driver

Private J. Jennings, Motor Transport, Army Service Corps, Stoke Park Gardens, March 1916:

I am driving a motor ambulance and take my turn for going up to the advanced dressing stations every other night to bring back the wounded. We generally do two journeys in the night and, however dark it may be, we never have a light. It is very difficult to miss the holes made in the road by the shells.

I had a narrow escape some time back; the Germans appeared to know where we were and dropped their shells into us. Four of our fellows were wounded. I had a bullet through my overcoat that was hanging in the car; it had passed through the cushion of the car and had taken a piece of the hair stuffing and lodged it in a matchbox that was in my pocket. Two tires [*sic*] on my car were punctured by bullets, and the radiator was also hit. I can tell you I was glad when they finished and we got back a bit. But my little experiences are nothing to compare with some. I often think of the men that are gone from Stoke.

Construction Work in the Balkans

A Stoke Poges Soldier, February 1916:

We are making a road up through the mountains for our guns to get up, as it is all mule-tracks out here, and the road has to be done at once. I expect you will have seen in the papers where the line got damaged when the 10th Division and the French were retiring. We went and cleared the line and repaired the rail-road. This is going to be a rough job, as it is all hills, and the transport will be a trouble to get about. All we want is good weather, and then I think we shall make a show.

Will you please thank all kind friends in Stoke and Wexham for the parcel? They could not have sent anything better, and it arrived on Christmas Day.

Receipt of a Christmas Parcel

A Stoke Poges Sailor, February 1916:

I write to thank you all so very much for your great kindness and thought in sending me such a nice parcel. Everything will be most useful, and I appreciate it very much. We are all very happy and contented on board, but the weather we are having is miserable.

Within five minutes from when I received the parcel the pudding was in boiling water, and I had it for supper, and it was excellent – couldn't have been better, so my mess mates said, and quite right too. It passed expectations all together.

Whose Pudding for Christmas?

Private Albert Groves, Motor Transport, Army Service Corps, Wexham Street, March 1916:

I write to thank the people of Stoke and Wexham very much for the parcel they sent me.

Our officers are trying to buy a pig for our Christmas dinner, and I think our cooks are going to try and make us a plum pudding. But I am going to keep the one in my parcel in case the one they make us is no improvement on the ones they have made us before sometimes.

Facing the Bulgarians in the Balkans

A Stoke Poges Soldier, April 1916.
Letter dated 28 January 1916:

I expect by this time Stoke is a bit quiet, most of the men being called up. We don't get much news out here till it is fifteen days old.

We are quite ready for any advance that might come along. My platoon are holding the extreme right of our Division, and we have got a box seat I can tell you. I don't give much for the Bulgars or anyone else's chance that might try and move us. I don't think myself that they will try to get to Salonika. You can guess what sort of position we are in when to get there we have to climb about 1,200 feet, and then we have a good field of fire – about eight miles of plain-in front of us.

We have had a lot of snow, and it was very bad for a few days, as it drifted a lot and you could not see where you were falling into. I am glad to say it is melting away. The sun rises about 7.30 a.m., and it is warm in the daytime but very severe frosts at night. You can tell what it is like in the day, as we were bathing in the Lake – the other day. Will you please thank all the friends in Stoke Poges and Wexham, and also Mr Mowatt, for the parcel, which I received quite safely?

Lance-Corporal Bottle is well. I have also seen Private C.E. Mitchell, and he was well. I have not seen Driver W. Swabey since I wrote last. They are on our left a long way off.

Sergeant Pargeter writes from the Balkan Front

Sergeant William Pargeter, 1st Battalion, Royal Scots, Stoke Common, April 1916:

We are up in the hills, making roads and digging trenches and living in bivouacs. The enemy are over the frontier, and the Greeks are between them and us. I don't think they will worry us much as the country is very hilly, and not easy for moving big guns. It is very quiet here. When we were in Salonika we used to be visited by hostile airmen occasionally. They dropped one bomb on our camp and blew up a tent, but without injuring anyone.

I am very sorry to say we buried our Battalion Sergeant-Major today. His dug-out fell in on the top of him, and he died before he could be got out, and is our first casualty on this front.*

Repulsing an Enemy Attack

Gunner William Gutteridge, Royal Field Artillery, Farnham Road, April 1916.

Letter dated 24 February 1916:

We are having very cold weather here, snow and frost, and the roads are very slippery.

There has been a very heavy bombardment here; the Germans dropped some thousand shells on a redoubt here in an hour, and then launched an attack by infantry. We opened fire immediately and caught them in crossfire as they were leaving their trenches. Our infantry told us our fire was very deadly and that the enemy's attack broke down half way between their trenches and our own.

One of our chaps is now putting a 'whizz-bang' to close examination. It dropped in a field close to us but did not explode. I would sooner he examined it than I, for the further I am away from these the better I like it.

An Enemy Attack

Private Edward Ware, 6th Battalion, Oxford and Bucks Light Infantry, Wexham Street, May 1916.

In November 1915 it was reported that he had been wounded in the jaw:

We were going to have a rest for Christmas but as the word came down to our officer that the Germans were going to attack us, that news put a stop to it.

Our boys were ready for them to come; we were longing to have another tug-of-war with them, as we know we can hold our own against them. They came in massed formation. That is the time to catch them; you could mow them down like corn – and they had had no mercy for our wounded comrades.

Life on the Balkan Front

A Stoke Poges Soldier, May 1916.

Letter dated 27 March 1916:

Many thanks for your letter, which I received yesterday, which I must say, was a good day for me. It was my birthday, and I had not received any letters for six weeks, and they all arrived yesterday – eleven in all and a good bag of papers. I have been away from the battalion in Hospital since the 7th.

---

* The 1st Battalion left Marseilles on 27 November 1915 on the troopship *Ionian* and anchored off Salonika 5 December 1915. The War Diary entry for 30 January 1916 records: 'at 10.30 a.m. Acting Sergt Major Williams was accidentally killed. He was constructing a 'dug out' when one of the roof supports broke & the roof … fell on top of him.' Aged 39 years, Joseph Edward Williams, who came from Blackpool, is buried in Mikra British Cemetery, Kalamaria.

I received a letter from Harry Hughes* yesterday, and he is well. I have not seen him. He put where he was, but Mr Censor saw it and marked it out. I have also seen some men from W. Gutteridge's† company, and I have sent him a note by a man who is going back from here.

I had one of my mates to see me yesterday. He walked 15 miles to here, and carried a sand bag full of tinned things that the sergeants of the Company and the platoon officer had got for me – fruit, salmon, butter, jam, and other things, and he had to get back the same night, so you can tell he was a brick.

I am pleased to see Mitchell and Dean‡ have got their promotion. It shows that Stoke and Wexham have got the right stuff in them to get on, as there are plenty waiting for these jobs.

Now I must tell you a little of what happened this morning. We generally get up about 6.30, but Mr German came this morning and called us. They took advantage of the clouds being low, so they were able to get well over before the guns from the harbour could find them. It was about 4.30 when they got here. One of their bombs caused a terrible explosion. You can guess what it dropped on.

I see in the Magazine there is a collection for a Motor Boat Ambulance for the wounded in Mesopotamia. I wish it every success. It will be much better for them to come down by water. When I came down to the Field Ambulance I had four miles to go on a stretcher fixed to two wheels with a mule to pull it along. It took me all my time to hang on, and I had all my strength, so I don't know how they will get the wounded down.

It is very dangerous on these tracks at night. If you get one wheel over the edge of the track your wheels slip and over goes the lot. We have seen limbers go over and over, dragging the mules with them, and finishing up in the ravine 80 feet below, so you can tell what the transport has to put up with in this country. Lance-Corporal Bottle§ was well on the 26th.

I hope you will see us all return to line up at Stoke – winners – say, before the Flower Show.

Herbert Banister's View of the Germans

Private Herbert Banister, 1st Battalion of the Duke of Cornwall's Light Infantry, Uxbridge Road, September 1916.

Herbert Banister who was reported the previous year as having received a shrapnel wound wrote:

The men were unable to get to us with the ammunition they were carrying and eventually there were only four of us left; a short while

---

* Sapper Harry Hughes from Stoke Green serving in the Royal Engineers.

† Walter Gutteridge, then a corporal, who, shortly after his promotion to sergeant, was killed in action 3 October 1916 in a battle to capture a village called Yenikeui in Northern Greece.

‡ Corporal A. Mitchell from Wexham Street was serving in the 2nd Battalion of the Oxford and Bucks Light Infantry and Bombardier W. Dean was in the 133rd Battery, Royal Field Artillery.

§ Lance-Corporal A. Bottle, from Sefton Park, was serving in the 8th Battalion of the Oxford and Bucks Light Infantry.

after the Corporal got wounded. We managed very well under the circumstances and were able to do a good bit while the supply of ammunition lasted. Then the other two men got hit, I being the only one left, and how I got back is hard to say. As soon as I did get back I was furnished with more ammunition and then it was easy work to mow them down as they came across the field towards us.

The German Army consists mostly of exceptionally young men or boys and of rather old men. I have seen but few middle-aged men. They all carry a number of bombs and throw quite freely, not caring as to whether the men are already helpless or not.

I saw it in the papers that the German officers are known to use whips on their men, little did I think I should see an actual instance, and what I did see was a number of men scrambling over a mass of wood and bricks beside a road and an officer on horseback lashed at them with his whip as men would lash a team of horses. He must certainly have been a hard-hearted beast, but one of the gunners I have heard since accounted for him. How different to our men, you would hardly credit their spirit or how they carried on as if it was simply a matter of course.

Sergeant F. Leslie, DCM

Sergeant Frederick Leslie, Royal Berkshire Regiment, Uxbridge Road, May 1917.

The Parish Magazine congratulated Sergeant F. Leslie on having been awarded the Distinguished Conduct Medal for gallantry in the field:

> We captured a village from Fritz, and there were two such lovely cats I had to stop and stroke them if I'd been shot. I should have liked them, but I had enough to do to get myself along, or I would have brought one back here.

As the editor commented 'his hard fighting has not made him hard hearted'.

Private Lavington's Ship is Torpedoed

Private F. Lavington, Army Service Corps, Framewood, October 1917.

The Parish Magazine reported that Private Lavington had been torpedoed:

> ... When about 130 miles off a certain coast, his ship was torpedoed, after two previous attempts which they managed to escape, about thirty men being killed. The rest took to the boats, and were drifting about eight hours when they were picked up by a vessel, and for eight days their rations were three biscuits per man per day until they were landed at a very distant port. They afterwards got back to England. The Captain of the U boat was quite a decent fellow and spoke good English. He told the English Captain he knew they had left port six and a half hours earlier than was expected, and what cargo they were carrying.

Brigadier-General R. Howard-Vyse Visits Jerusalem

Brigadier-General Richard Howard-Vyse CMG, DSO, Desert Mounted Corps in the Egyptian Expeditionary Force, Stoke Place, February 1918.

33 *Richard Howard-Vyse.*

Richard Howard-Vyse sent an account of his visit to Jerusalem:*

> Yesterday my General and I went up to the Holy City to spend the night. We are not allowed into any of the buildings inside the City, and I think quite rightly. So we could only look at them from outside. Jerusalem has a very thick wall; inside it is as dirty, as squalid, narrow, and crowded as all other Eastern towns I have visited. The Church of the Holy Sepulchre is not imposing from the outside, as the houses are crowded right up against it. The Mosque of Omar, which stands on the site of the Temple, is very beautiful. Outside the wall of it is a place where the Jews wail.
>
> Outside the walls of the City, every nation has thought it right to raise a monument to its piety in the shape of a Monastery, Church, or Hospital. The nicest one is the Russian, which is on the Mount of Olives. The most marvellous view from the top of it is right over the Jordan valley and the Dead Sea and the Moabite mountains beyond. Really lovely, except that at this time of year at any rate, it is all bare and stony. Jerusalem is 2,500 ft. above sea-level and the Dead Sea 1,300 ft. below it, so you can imagine what a view it is.
>
> All this country is marvellous for seeing. Not being able to go into the Holy Places, what interested me most was the wonderful view, the mixture of Jews and Russians and Arabs and Egyptians and all the shades in between, and the little narrow streets, most of them really arcades, built of solid stone with vaulted roofs. What impressed me most was the unworthiness of the whole place. We had an open-air service. Altogether it was rather a wonderful experience.

Sixteen Days in 'No-Man's Land'

Private Fred Spring, 5th Battalion, Oxford and Bucks Light Infantry, Stoke Green, March 1918.

34 *Fred Spring.*

Fred Spring was wounded in the attack on Hillside Work that formed part of the great British offensive which commenced on 3 May 1917 on a 12-mile front to the east of Arras. An artillery barrage to which the enemy responded with artillery and heavy and accurate machine gun fire preceded the attack. Fred was wounded in the advance and spent the next 16 days in 'No Man's Land'. Fred was in A Company and 75 of the 129 men became casualties.

---

* Allenby had entered Jerusalem on foot on 11 December 1917 'to avoid emulating the Kaiser's triumphant entry on horseback in 1898 ... No Allied flags were flown over the city, and to avoid offending Muslim tradition, Indian Muslim troops were sent to guard the Dome of the Rock.' Gilbert, Martin, *First World War*, 1994.

As a result of his wounds he was invalided out of the army. He was awarded a Silver War Badge.* These were worn in the coat lapel and stopped women from handing white feathers to men in civilian clothes who had served and been wounded. Fred returned to Stoke Green and wrote an account of his 16 days in 'No Man's Land' for the March 1918 issue of the Parish Magazine:

Dear Mr Editor

You said you would like to have an account of my experience of 16 days lying out in 'No Man's Land', which I can assure you was a most weird and unpleasant one.

Our Company went up to the trenches on the 2nd May 1917, and about 12 of us went on patrol all night and came back at 3 a.m. to report, and then we made an attack on Fritz.

I was wounded just after half-past 3, while running across to get at Fritz, and was shot twice through the leg, one bullet passing through and one staying in, causing a compound fracture. I crawled in a shell-hole close by, and there I lay, with several more, until night fell, when they all crawled away except three of us, one with his foot nearly off, one wounded in the leg and back, and myself.

We waited and prayed that stretcher-bearers might find us and pick us up, but nobody came until three days afterwards, when a Sergeant found us. He told us he would send us help and that the RAMC was coming to search for us. But as he was speaking to us the shelling was fast and furious, and there did not seem much chance of anyone reaching us, as both sides were sweeping the ground with shells, so we kept each other as cheerful as we could. What little food we had we were obliged to be very careful with, but water seemed to be the worst trouble. We had none for days; in fact I never tasted water for eight days.

After eight days of weary waiting in the first shell-hole, two of us said we would try and crawl in to our lines. So while I was getting out of the shell-hole the other one crawled a little way and found half-a-bottle of water and a 'Maconochie',† which we gave to the one with his foot nearly off. We then started off and got about 50 yards when my mate said he could go no further, and we found nothing to eat and drink. Soon I saw a poor fellow about 20 yards away, and decided to see what he had on him, but when I got to him I found nothing, so crawled a little further to another, and found three-parts of a bottle of water and a little food. I had some difficulty to find my mate in the shell-hole again, and just as I got back and safely in, machine gun bullets came whistling right over the shell-hole, so Fritz must have seen me and it made me feel jolly queer I can tell you.

* The Silver War Badge was authorised in September 1916 and takes the form of a circular badge with the legend 'For King and Empire – Services Rendered' surrounding the George V cypher. The badge was awarded to all military personnel who were discharged as a result of sickness or wounds contracted or received during the war, either at home or overseas.

† The 'Maconochie', named after the manufacturer, was a round sealed tin, 6in. in diameter and 2in. deep, containing a meat and vegetable meal.

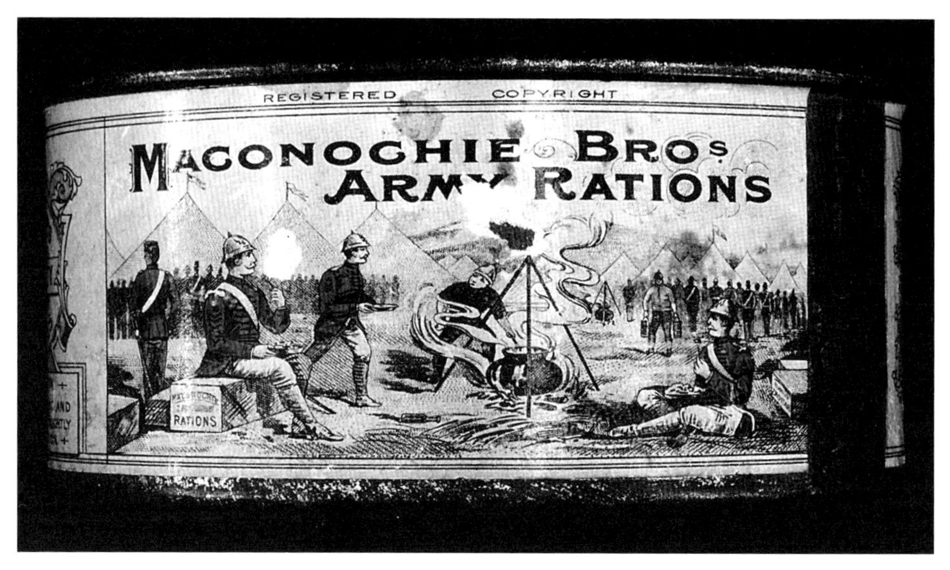

35 *Maconochie. IWM photograph.*

We decided to stay where we were for one more night and try our luck the next night, but we still felt too weak and ill, so we had to stop four days with only the three-parts of a bottle of water. My mate then said that he felt better and would try to get in, but I am sorry to say that half-an-hour later the poor fellow died. So I stayed there until 10 o'clock at night and then tried to crawl in, but what with the shelling and the shell-holes I made no headway, but only kept knocking my leg against great clods of clay, which caused me intense pain and made me feel ill.

I stopped for a rest in another shell-hole, in which were two more chums, and I found a bottle of water and a little food on one of them. It seemed little enough, and I had to look at it to see whether I dare eat any. I managed to make it last by allowing myself about three dessert spoonsful a day and eating grass and dandelions in between whiles. Thank God it rained one day, and I was able to catch one bottle of water, which lasted me until the night I got picked up.

Fritz was on the lookout all the while for moving objects, and he spotted a patrol of ours, and there was a tidy old dust-up for a while. At 10 o'clock that night I felt as if I ought to make a last attempt to find our trenches, which I thought lay about 300 to 400 yards away, so I started to crawl along as best I could. It was slow progress, and my leg pained cruelly, but I stuck it, and reached our lines at 2 a.m.

They then gave me something warm to eat and drink and made me as comfortable as they could for the time being, and by stages I got to hospital and from there to Blighty. It seemed good to see the trees and flowers once more instead of ruin and havoc everywhere. I could write a lot more, but I am afraid I have made it too long as it is, so will dry up.

A Christmas Parcel reaches Palestine

Sergeant Fred Hartley, Sanitation Corps, RAMC, Stoke Green, April 1918:

36 *Fred Hartley.*

> We are most grateful for the kindness shown, the pudding is already in a mess tin on the fire. I am now in the Judean Hills outside Jerusalem. For the last twelve months our duties have been the purification and service of drinking water. Some of the wells are most picturesque and interesting. The natives used a wooden wheel which pulled up the endless chain of buckets worked by oxen or a camel; we use power pumps. We were flooded out at Christmas, but managed to get a stew by the evening, which was most welcome after 'iron rations'.

The Value of Keeping in Touch

Lance Corporal George Isbell, Army Service Corps, Uxbridge Road, April 1918:

> I am sitting on a hill overlooking the Golden City while writing this. We pass right through the City every day. Whoever thought that I should see it. Very many thanks to Stoke Poges for the splendid parcel. The pudding was A1. I always look forward to the Parish Magazine. It keeps one in touch with the dear old village. Everyone in Stoke is doing their share, even the school children. I feel that no other village can be doing better. There are quite a number of our Boys out here, but I have only met two, viz., H. Elderfield and W. Beech.

The Armistice

Private John Tarrant, Coldstream Guards, Uxbridge Road, January 1919:

37 *John Tarrant.*

> When the armistice came we were in a large town. The people there were very enthusiastic over the soldiers as they arrived, and they had great rejoicings and plenty of decorations. Since then we have had considerable marches, and we are now in another well-known town in Belgium. It is the same here, plenty of flags and great rejoicings.
>
> The people must have hidden a great deal of their goods from the Germans, for the gold and silver and other articles of which Germany is short are plentiful enough here now.
>
> I have seen a good many returned British prisoners making their way back to France en route for England, having been released by the Germans. They look pretty bad and have had a rough time. I do not expect to be home for some time yet, but of course I do not know anything for certain.

The Surrender of the German Fleet

Boy Telegraphist A. Fleet, HMS Lion, *Holly Bush Hill, January 1919:*

We left our berth just outside the Forth Bridge at 3.30 on the Thursday morning, and proceeded out to the rendezvous. I had an excellent opportunity of seeing the scene, as the old *Lion* led the Red Fleet or starboard division. The Fleet was divided into two portions, the Red and the Blue Fleet. The *Queen Elizabeth* was leading the Blue Fleet.

38 *HMS* Lion.

The course we were steering would bring us (the Red Fleet) on one side of the Germans and the Blue Fleet on the other so that in case of their showing fight they would be caught between two fires. The crews were all at action stations, and on every side one could hear 'Will they fight?' Well, at 9.30 the men who happened to be on the upper deck caught sight of the German High Sea Fleet coming over the horizon, with one of our cruisers, the *Cardiff*, leading them. Our Fleets then closed about them, and we turned and shaped our courses forward toward the Forth. It was a never to be forgotten sight, the pride of the German Navy, crestfallen and defeated, surrendering without any remonstrance. It was a degrading scene to see the ships the Grand Fleet had been hunting for and waiting for four years refuse to give them the fight that would have repaid all the waiting and watching.

Here and there a few small steamers crowded with spectators were to be seen. Just opposite the *Lion* was her old opponent the *Derflinger.* Farther down the line can be seen the notorious *Bayern* and *Seidlitz.*

Leading the German Fleet are the five battle cruisers, then come the nine battleships, then the seven light cruisers, and far astern are the 49 destroyers. Over the German column a British naval airship is flying, while here and there aeroplanes belonging to the battleships are to be seen. Besides the aeroplane-ships proper, most of our large ships carry one or more aeroplanes for scouting and range finding duties.

As we near the mouth of the Forth our ships gradually close round the Germans, until they finally drop anchor in a place selected for them off Inchkeith.

Then our Grand Fleet moves back into their original berths inside the harbour, leaving our Second Battle Squadron to keep guard over the Germans.

The final ceremony has yet to be performed. As the *Queen Elizabeth* slowly passes to her berth, the crews of the ships assemble on the upper deck, and three hearty cheers are given by each ship as the Admiral passes.

On board HMS *Lion* the word is passed round that Beatty is coming aboard to address the men of the *Lion* and First Battle Cruiser Squadron at 10 on Sunday morning.

39 Bayern.

40 Seidlitz.

41 Derflinger.

The speech is to the effect that the First Battle Cruiser Squadron has been chosen to escort the German Battle Cruisers to their last resting place, also congratulating it on its great work during the war. It is of no small interest that he ends up with saying that leave is coming at the earliest possible moment. When the Admiral has gone, the *Lion* quietly moves out of harbour to where the German Battle Cruisers are awaiting her.

Following the *Lion* came the *Repulse, Renown, Princess Royal,* and *Tiger.* The order of the Fleet is thus – the *Lion* leading the line, the five Germans following in line ahead, with the *Repulse* and *Renown* on one side, and the *Tiger* and *Princess Royal* on the other.

At 6 the next morning land is sighted, and we proceed into the harbour at Scapa Flow. Here the German ships are to remain until peace is actually signed and it is decided to what use they shall be put.

Chapter Four

The Assault on the Petit Couronne

A Hill Too Far for Henry Dancer, Henry Fleet and Frederick King

One of the many tragedies of the Great War was the impact the loss of life had on communities when men from the same villages, towns and counties served together in the same regiments and battalions of those regiments. The deaths of so many men, including brothers, from the same area in one battle was devastating for their communities.

Although Stoke Poges men served in a great diversity of regiments, including 16 in the Royal Navy, the largest number in one regiment served in the various battalions of the Oxfordshire and Buckinghamshire Light Infantry. Fortunately although the number was about 45, it was not a significant proportion of the total of 306 men. Nevertheless, nine of the men who lost their lives were in the Oxfordshire and Buckinghamshire Light Infantry and three of them died in the same battle.

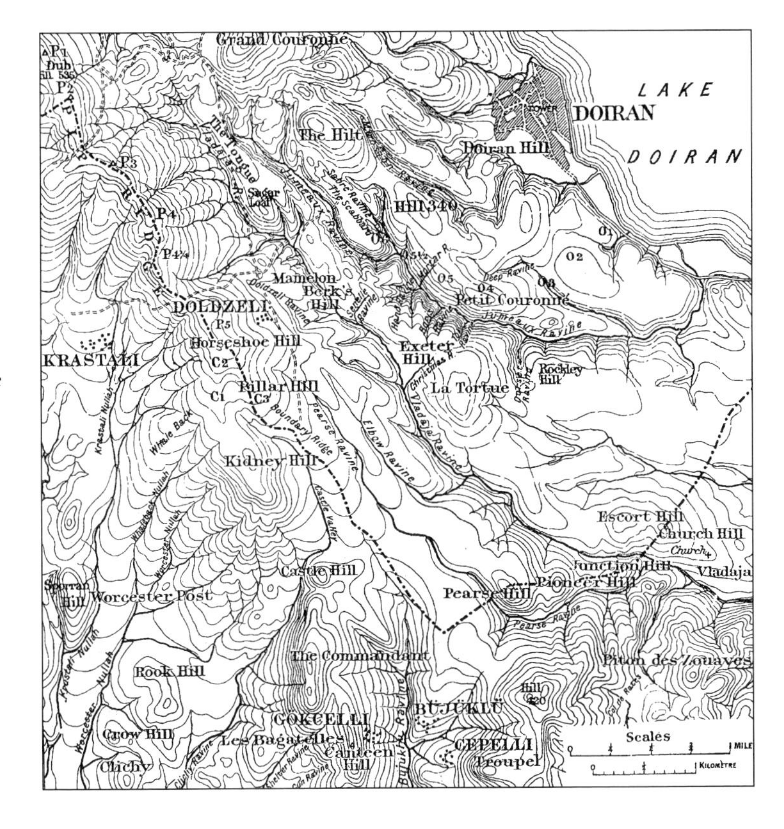

42 *Map of the Doiran Sector.*

The comradeship and friendship of men from the same village serving together is reflected in the letters they sent home. This is very apparent in the letters from those in the Oxfordshire and Buckinghamshire Light Infantry.

News was communicated in letters from home and via the Parish Magazine sent to sons and husbands. The loss of Frederick King, Henry Dancer and Henry Fleet in the same battle, on the same day, 7 May 1917, fighting with the 7th Battalion in Salonika, would have been received with great sadness, especially as two of them were born and educated in the village. This battle in a remote corner of Europe, fought by what has been called Britain's forgotten army, deserves a separate chapter in an account of Stoke Poges men in the Great War.

The 7th Service Battalion (meaning war service only) was formed from volunteers to Kitchener's new army at Cowley Barracks, Oxford, in September 1914. Frederick King was one of those volunteers. The 7th Battalion, together with the 7th Royal Berkshire Regiment, 11th Worcestershire Regiment and 9th Gloucestershire Regiment, became part of 78th Infantry Brigade, 26th Division. The 8th Battalion of the Oxford and Bucks became the Pioneer Battalion to this Division at the same time and Stoke Poges men served in it.

After service in France from September to November 1915, the 26th Division embarked for Salonika (today called Thessalonika) where it established a defensive line five miles north of Salonika Harbour, which became known as the 'Birdcage Line'. Training continued in the early months of 1916 and the Pioneer Battalion was employed in road construction supporting the work of the Royal Engineers. In July 1916 the Division moved to the north to the Doiran Sector. This consisted of a line of foothills, about 13 miles long, running east to west from the southern tip of Lake Doiran to the river Vardar. Opposing them were the Bulgarian 1st and 2nd Armies. As the Regimental Chronicle for 1916 records:

> These hills averaging some 900 feet in height, are absolutely treeless, though covered with scrub, usually dwarf, prickly leaved, evergreen oak, and their slopes are seamed with deep, steep-sided ravines. Away in the distance stood the great peak known as Grand Couronne, which for the next three years, was to be the evil eye of our existence, for not only could it see every movement in our front line, but it over-looked our lines of communication, our railroads, our aerodromes, and even the Aegean forty miles away.

The 7th Battalion's section of the line was opposite the 1,900-feet-high Grand Couronne. It dominated and overlooked the country for many miles and this was to be the 26th Division's battleground and home for the next two-and-a-half years.

> On 29 July 1916, the 7th Battalion took over a section of trenches occupied by French troops and immediately began sending out patrols at night. On the night of 17/18 August, the Battalion attacked a feature known as 'Horseshoe Hill'. After considerable difficulties and fighting off Bulgar counter-attacks, the position was taken and held. They became the first British troops to gain a foothold into Serbia.
>
> For the next eight months, the British held the western end of the line in the Balkans. With allied reinforcements of Serbian, Italian and Russian troops, offensive operations began in earnest and these culminated in the fall of Monastir to French and Serbian forces in November 1916.

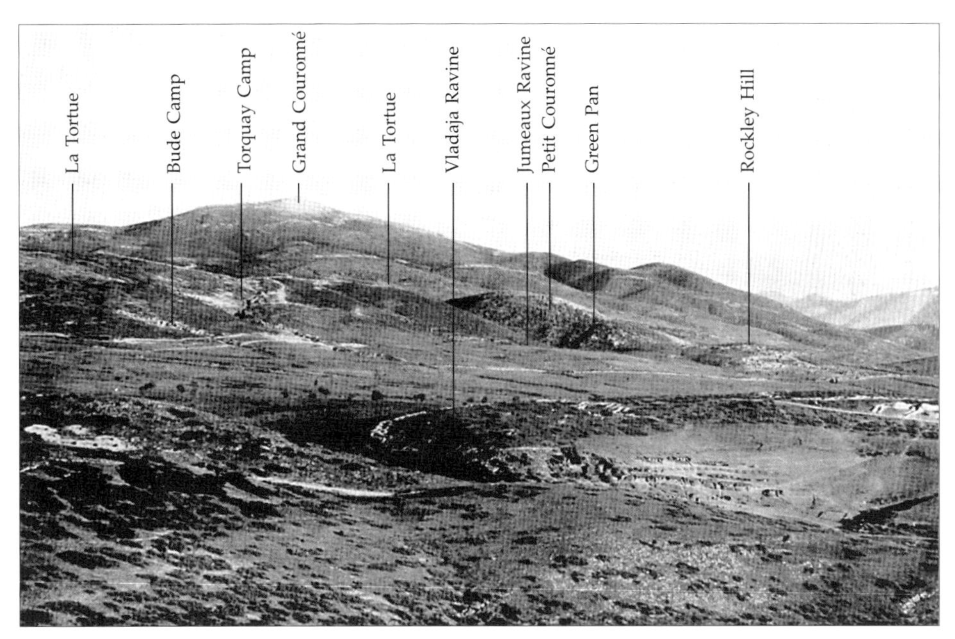

43 *Grand and Petit Couronne.*

> For the 7th Battalion this period consisted of short spells in the front-line trenches followed by frequent moves to various camps as part of the Divisional or Brigade Reserve. Front-line duty was a routine round of night patrols into No Man's Land and improving the defences, which could only be achieved by hacking through the solid rock. All day and everyday the enemy bombarded the British lines, which sometimes affected the Battalion. Casualties, though light compared with those in France and Flanders, were persistent. The winter of 1916-17 was also severe with heavy rain and snow which seeped into the trenches and dugouts and then froze.*

Henry Dancer who had enlisted in December 1915, and Henry Fleet who had enlisted in June 1916, both reached Salonika and were with the 7th Battalion by Christmas 1916. Henry Dancer wrote home that he was in the trenches up to his waist in mud and water.

The British Salonika Force failed to dislodge the Bulgarian 1st Army at what was to be known as the First Battle of Lake Doiran, 24/25 April and 8/9 May 1917.

The first general attack was made on the night of 24 April by the 26th Division on the right and the 22nd Division on the left. The intention was to take the Bulgarian front-line position that ran along the Grand Couronne and a ridge running north and south known as Hill 535. The position also included the hill Petit Couronne that was the key to the Bulgarian front line and the town of Doiran.

---

* *The Oxfordshire & Buckinghamshire Light Infantry, The Great War 1914-1919, 7th (Service) Battalion.* An account written by Dino Lemonofides, Research and Archive Team, The Oxfordshire and Buckinghamshire Light Infantry Museum.

Whilst the 22nd Division was successful, the attack by the 26th Division failed with heavy casualties. The terrain was difficult, not helped by darkness, and it was impossible to keep the men supplied. The British were outnumbered and the Bulgarians with their listening sets heard practically everything spoken over the British telephones.

The second attack by the 26th Division was on 8/9 May. The 77th Brigade was to take all the enemy front-line positions between Petit Couronne and the Lake. If successful, the 7th Battalion would assault the eastern and higher bump of Petit Couronne. This was separated from the hill where the British line lay by a deep ravine called the Jumeaux Ravine. Although the trenches of the two sides were only 600 yards apart as the crow flies, the distance by the shortest path was some 2,000 yards. The attack took place even though 77th Brigade failed in its objectives.

In his account Captain C.A.Salvesen, who commanded D Company, described the route taken in the attack:

> A Company went out well to the right, and doubled, by an almost precipitous track, down into a very steep but dry ravine, which ran between their positions and that of the enemy. This was crossed, and the ascent of the other side began. B Company went out by a gap on the left and doubled down, through thick brushwood, by a track made and used previously by the Bulgars. This track was the only possible way through the undergrowth. During the whole time the company was passing through the gap the enemy kept up a slow barrage-fire with shrapnel.

The plan was to assault the Bulgar position at five minutes before midnight after a ten-minute bombardment. Just before the assault enemy heavy trench mortar shells landed amongst the two companies. As they waited for the British bombardment to lift, casualties continued to be fairly heavy. The bombardment lifted and the first enemy position was taken. During the ten-minute wait for the second British bombardment to lift, the Bulgar barrage of heavy, medium, and light mortar shells, and of artillery of calibres up to eight-inch guns, descended on the captured position. Casualties were severe. Counter-attacks by the enemy along a communications trench were repulsed.

Salvesen's account continued:

> When the attack on the Bulgar support line was launched, the casualties in A, B and C Companies had reached well over 40 per cent of their original strength, and only three officers out of twelve were able to go on. D Company had been moved up into close support and suffered heavy casualties also. The attack on the Bulgar support line was successful on the right, but on the left no more than a temporary footing was ever gained. This gain could not be held.

Counter-attacks drove the Battalion back to the old Bulgar front line. Between this time, 12.10 a.m. until 5 a.m., five or six counter-attacks were repulsed. Only 60 to 70 men fit to fight remained; all the officers and a large proportion of the NCOs were casualties.

At 5 a.m. three companies of the 7th Berkshires were sent in to attack the enemy support line without success. At 7 a.m. the C.O. (Lieut-Colonel Robinson) arrived to check the situation. Orders to withdraw came at 9 a.m. but the withdrawal was not made until it was established that the Berkshires could not hold the position. The Berkshires organised the withdrawal, no officer of the Battalion being left and the C.O. having been wounded. By 9.30 a.m., when the evacuation was being made, there were nearly one hundred stretcher cases with only two routes back, both being continuously shelled. It took until 3 p.m. to complete the evacuation.

As Major Riley's diary records:

> None of those who were still in the trenches and camps on Tortue Hill will ever forget the endless stream of wounded officers and men coming back from Petit Couronne. The procession began in the early hours of the morning, and continued until darkness had fallen. At about 10 a.m. Lieut-Colonel Robinson came down mortally wounded, supported by Father Day the Roman Catholic Padre.

Out of 600 men, six officers and 105 other ranks were killed and 10 officers and 349 other ranks wounded. Sergeant Frederick King and Privates Henry Dancer and Henry Fleet from Stoke Poges were among those killed.

In the Battalion History an officer writes of the battle:

> Reviewed from a military point of view, no conclusion can be arrived at but that the action completely failed to accomplish its purpose. Not an inch of ground had been gained, yet, presuming that the attack was bound to take place for reasons beyond our ken, we could not help feeling a certain satisfaction at the way in which we had attempted and almost accomplished a nearly impossible operation – how nearly impossible one could only realise when actually walking over the ground after the Armistice.

The Commonwealth War Graves Commission in its historical information writes of those commemorated:

> From October, 1915 to the end of November, 1918, the British Salonika Force suffered some 2,800 deaths in action, 1,400 from wounds and 4,200 from sickness. The campaign in which they fought was one in which few successes were gained, and none of any importance could be gained by them until the last two months. Their action was hampered throughout by widespread and unavoidable sickness (the British forces which attacked in September, 1918 had less than half their normal establishment present); by continual diplomatic and personal differences with neutrals or allies; by the presence on one front of a wide malarial river valley and on the other of difficult mountain ranges; and by the necessity of constructing by far the greater part of the roads and railways which it used. It overcame all difficulties, but this Memorial indicates the cost.

Henry Dancer's body is buried in the cemetery. Henry Fleet and Frederick King are commemorated on the marble panels sunk in the piers of the obelisk, but there are graves of unidentified soldiers in the cemetery.

Chapter Five

Gallantry and other Awards

Two of the three most senior officers from Stoke Poges at the end of the war, Brigadier-General Richard Howard-Vyse and Lieutenant-Colonel Frederick Allhusen, were both awarded the Distinguished Service Order and made Companions of the Order of St Michael and St George. Frederick Allhusen, who resided at Fulmer House, Fulmer, was the brother of Henry Allhusen of Stoke Court. The third officer was Lieutenant-Colonel Lord Decies of Sefton Park, but he was awarded his Distinguished Service Order during the South African War.

The Military Cross was awarded to two officers and a Distinguished Conduct Medal and ten Military Medals to other ranks.

Military Cross

Captain Martin Bowen, 1st Battalion, Oxford and Bucks Light Infantry, was awarded the Military Cross for his part in the capture of Tombois Farm on 16 and 17 April 1917. The citation reads 'For conspicuous gallantry and devotion to duty. He led his company in the most gallant manner, and in spite of very difficult conditions succeeded in gaining his objective. He set a fine example to his men.' *London Gazette, Supplement*, 18 June 1917, page 5985.

Captain Alan Walmsley, Royal Welsh Fusiliers, was awarded the Military Cross for 'Gallant and Distinguished Conduct in the Field', *London Gazette, Supplement*, 14 January 1916, page 586. He was not decorated by the King until 14 November 1916 because of the time needed for him to recover from his wounds. He was wounded twice in 1914 and at Loos in September 1915.

Distinguished Conduct Medal

Acting Quarter Master Sergeant F. Leslie, Princess Charlotte of Wales's (Royal Berkshire Regiment), was awarded the Distinguished Conduct Medal in May 1917. The citation reads 'Sergeant (Acting C.Q.M.S) F. Leslie For conspicuous gallantry and devotion to duty. He rendered invaluable assistance to his Company Commander throughout, and was largely responsible for the success of the operations.' *London Gazette*, 11 May 1917, page 4596. Frederick Leslie first enlisted in April 1900. He was used to train one of the Kitchener battalions between August 1914 and early 1915. Later he joined the 2nd Battalion of the Royal Berkshire Regiment.

Military Medal

Signalman Henry Beasley, 9th Fusiliers, received his award for gallant conduct on 6 April 1918 during operations north of Albert. *London Gazette, Supplement*,

16 July 1918, page 8311. Henry Beasley married Dorothy Freeman of School Lane, Stoke Poges, 14 March 1918.

Sergeant-Major James Fitz Gibbons, of the 4th and later the 56th Australian Battalion, was an early volunteer who fought in German New Guinea, and Gallipoli where he was wounded at Lone Pine. In February 1916, after Gallipoli, survivors from the 4th and fresh reinforcements from Australia were formed into the 56th Battalion. Both battalions consisted of men mainly from New South Wales. The 56th fought on the Somme, notably in the battle at Fromelles. James Gibbons was wounded a second time and awarded the Military Medal. He married Alice Jane Turner of Hockley Hole, Stoke Poges, 3 February 1917.

Private Arthur Gutteridge, Oxford and Bucks Light Infantry, won his award in March 1918. *London Gazette, Supplement*, 13 March 1918, page 3234. Arthur had five brothers who served, one of whom Walter was killed in Salonika in 1916.

Bombardier A.E. Lowe, Royal Garrison Artillery, was awarded his medal for conspicuous bravery in the field whilst under heavy shellfire, *London Gazette, Supplement*, 21 August 1917, page 8644. The Parish Magazine in August 1917 records this note about Lowe who came from Wexham Street: 'Previous to this war he was in the 'Fighting Fifth', and served in the West Indies and South Africa five years. He re-enlisted early in 1915, and went to France early in 1916 with the Oxfordshire Heavy Battery. He lost his brother Walter last year, and has another brother in France. Mrs Lowe has three brothers in the Navy, two in the Army in France and one badly wounded and discharged. A fine record.'

Lance-Corporal C. Moore, Royal Engineers, received his award for conspicuous bravery in the field, *London Gazette*, 11 January 1918, page 14. C. Moore was the son-in-law of Mr Brock of Wexham Street.

Private D. Nicholls, Royal Army Medical Corps. The Parish Magazine of December 1917 records: 'He has had some very narrow escapes when bringing in the wounded. On one occasion he found two men in a shell hole where they had been for two days, and while helping them he heard sounds from a third man calling for help. It was found that the cries came from a deep well, at the bottom of which the poor fellow was up to his neck in mud. Nicholls had to go a long way back to get a rope and help, and after five hours got the man to the surface, shells falling in the neighbourhood all the time. It appeared that being heavily shelled the man had jumped into what he thought to be a shell hole, but what proved to be a disused well.' For this Nicholls received the Military Medal, *London Gazette, Supplement*, 12 December 1917, page 13018.

44 *Sergeant Percy Plumridge, MM.*

Sergeant Percy Plumridge, 1/1st Bucks Battalion, Oxford and Bucks Light Infantry, was awarded the Military Medal for his part in the action on the night of 26/27 August 1918 when his battalion raided the Austrian trenches in the area of Sec and Ave on the Asiago Plateau. Percy was then a corporal. On 29 August 1918 Lieut-General the Earl of Cavan, the British Commander-in-Chief in Italy, presented decorations to men involved in the raid, including Percy. *London Gazette, Supplement*, 21 January 1919, page 23.

Private A.M. Tyson, Army Service Corps. Archibald Tyson was an ambulance driver who was awarded his medal in December 1917. *London Gazette, Supplement*, 13 March 1918, page 3247. He came to live in Stoke Poges after the war and died in 1920 as a result of his wounds and is buried in St Giles' Churchyard.

45 *Sergeant C.W. Webb, MM.*

Gunner S. Way, Tank Corps, was the church organist and the Parish Magazine reported in September 1918 that he 'was selected for service on a 'tank', the first Stoke man we believe to serve in one of these ungainly monsters'. He was awarded the Military Medal for his work on tanks, *London Gazette, Supplement*, 16 July 1918, page 8330.

Sergeant C.W. Webb, Royal Berkshire Regiment, 19 Farnham Road, who first enlisted in 1903, was wounded five times. He was the first Stoke Poges man to win the Military Medal. It was awarded for conspicuous bravery in the fighting of 27 and 28 July 1916, *London Gazette, Supplement*, 21 October 1916, page 10222. The award was announced on 28 October 1916 and presented at an awards ceremony held in the Victoria Barracks, Portsmouth, in February 1917 when 15 medals were presented to Royal Berkshire men for gallantry in the field. In November 1916, when Charles Webb was wounded for a second time, a bullet passed within an inch of his heart.

Chapter Six

Where They Lived in the Village

Although Bells Hill was the centre of the village, other settlements were also of importance including Stoke Green, Wexham Street, West End and the houses adjoining Stoke Common.

Bells Hill

46 *At the foot of Bells Hill was the Village Hall, built in 1912, and opened on 22 January 1913 with a smoking concert to which every man in the village over 15 was invited.*

47 *Looking up Bells Hill, c.1910, the first house was occupied by Mr Farley, seen here standing outside his gate. Miss Bailey the school mistress lived in one of the cottages further up the hill, and next to these cottages was Horace Newell's baker's shop where Thomas Trinder baked the bread. The white-walled building was the* Six Bells *public house that later had an extension built onto the front. The protruding building consisted of two shops, the first of which was James Harman the butcher, and the house where the Birch family lived.*

48 *A pre-1914 view looking south down Bells Hill from the Post Office and Squibb's General Store to the end terraced house where the Birch family lived.*

49 *This 1910 photograph shows the top of Bells Hill just above the junction with Uxbridge Road (Hollybush Hill). James Clayton, who served in the Army Service Corps, and Tom Barlow, with Devening's baker's shop at the end, owned the first two cottages. Where the two boys are standing was the cycle shop of Bert Burgess. The* Sefton Arms *was the building next to where the two ladies are standing. Behind these properties were cottages, one of which was occupied by the Gutteridge family, six of whose sons joined the army, including Walter who died in Salonika. In all 22 men from Bells Hill served.*

Uxbridge Road

The first house on the corner of Bells Hill and Uxbridge Road, not shown in the photograph opposite, was the post office where Mr Cook was the post-master. One of his postmen was Frank Reynolds who lost his life in the war.

Mrs Isbell and Mrs Hinge, the haberdasher, occupied two of the three cottages in the photograph. George Isbell joined the Essex Regiment and his brother Albert Edward joined the 2nd Battalion of the Oxford and Bucks Light Infantry, whilst their neighbour's son, Henry Hinge, served in the RAMC.

George Isbell was the assistant scoutmaster and he is in the photograph of the Stoke Poges Scout troop (see page 3) taken in 1911. In the summer of 1913 he was in charge of the advance party travelling to the troop's summer camp at Thursley in Surrey. George recounted the following incident for the Parish Magazine:

50 *Alf Gutteridge.*

51 *Ernie Gutteridge.*

> At Guildford our party had to change trains, and, while waiting, rendered a pecuniary assistance to a distinguished gentleman who, by way of recognition, handed his card to Assistant Scout Master G. Isbell. On the back of the card is pencilled as follows: 'This is to certify that in buying papers at Guildford platform I upset a handful of loose silver, all picked up and handed to me at once by scouts of Stoke Poges Troop – Rudyard Kipling.' A very weighty testimonial to the readiness of our scouts to assist the distressed.

The first of the two protruding semi-detached houses beyond the first three cottages was the home of the Betts family. Albert Betts, 4th Reserve Battalion, Oxford and Bucks Light Infantry, was wounded and taken prisoner 23 March 1918.

The Hazell and Brown families lived in the next two cottages, located just before the *Rose and Crown* public house. Lance-Corporal George Hazell, twice wounded, served in the Wiltshire Regiment and his brother Harry, also wounded, was in the 1/1st Battalion of the Oxford and Bucks Light Infantry. Following his

52 *Uxbridge Road.*

53 *Harry Hazell.*

hospitalisation after being wounded in July 1916, Harry was home on leave and this prompted a comment in the Parish Magazine: 'His powers of persuasion must have been great to convince the military authorities two years ago that he was then 18 years of age; he hardly looks more now. Anyhow there can be no doubt of his patriotism.' The records show that he was born in July or August 1898 so that when he enlisted on 12 April 1915 it was before his 17th birthday. He was probably the youngest to volunteer from Stoke Poges. He is shown in the photograph of the scout camp of 1911. Sadly, his son, also named Harry, lost his life in 1942 in the Second World War serving on the convoys to Russia.

Beyond the *Rose and Crown* the Banister and Robinson families lived in two cottages since demolished and now the *Rose and Crown* car park. Four of the Banister sons from Uxbridge Road served in the army. Herbert was a corporal in the Duke of Cornwall's Light Infantry, John and Arthur were in the Army Service Corps and Wilfred in the Rifle Brigade. Tom Collison was the half-brother of the four Banister boys and he died from a shell wound on 29 April 1918. Arthur, who was an ambulance driver, saw Tom after the shelling when he was wounded.

Wexham Street

Forty-one men from Wexham Street are listed in the Parish Magazine's list of those serving in the forces and this must have been from both sides of the road.

Sergeant Arthur Grey King lost his life in 1915 at the age of 42 when HM Cruiser *Bayano* was torpedoed. His mother lived in Rose Cottages. A neighbour was Private Edward Hancock of 3 Rose Cottages, who was invalided in 1918, when 42, having served in India with the Oxford and Bucks Light Infantry.

Two other men from Wexham Street were invalided out of the army, Sapper Arthur James who died of an incurable disease at the age of 46 in 1918 and Sapper George Evered who also died in 1918. Both are buried in St Giles' Churchyard. George Didcock also died in France in the great influenza pandemic of 1918.

54 *Robert Alsford, who died on 4 November 1918, just before the war ended, and his brother Frederick, lived in Rex Cottages, as did Private Alfred Grant.*

55 *Rose Cottages, in Wexham Street.*

56 *There were three public houses in Wexham Street, all on the Stoke Poges side, and Tom Collison was born in one of them, the* Stag, *in 1885 before his mother married William Banister. Arthur Gibbons from the* Stag *was in the Gloucestershire Regiment.*

57 *The* Plough *is one of the oldest public houses in the parish. Before the sixth bell was hung in St Giles' tower in 1830 it had been up ended on sacks of wheat in the pub and filled with beer.*

58 *The* Travellers Friend *stood in Wexham Street between the Plough and the Stag but it was demolished in the 1990s and replaced with houses.*

West End

The West End of 1910 is recognisable today. In the photograph, the first house on the right with the bicycle belonged to George and Fanny Gale three of whose sons served in the war. William in the Royal Berkshire Regiment died of wounds on 12 March 1917. His younger brothers Bert (Bucks Battalion, Oxford and Bucks Light Infantry) and Arthur (Royal Navy) both survived.

Number 2, West End, the next house in the photograph with the lady at the doorway, was the home of the Baldwin family. W.H. Baldwin was a boot maker and postman. He and his wife Mary had two sons in the army: Utton Edward, born in 1887, joined the Cheshire Regiment and Albert Ernest, born 1895, joined the 1/1st Bucks Battalion of the Oxford and Bucks Light Infantry.

The house with the ivy is Winterclyde. It had been a public house called the *Oddfellows Arms* but was closed in 1899 when the new *Dog and Pot* was built in Rogers Lane. There was no piped water then and all water had to be carried from the pump seen outside Winterclyde.

59 *West End, 1910.*

60 *South Hill Cottages.*

Further along next to Winterclyde, but set back, are Gladstone Cottages, which still exist. Lieutenant Archibald Wareham, Durham Light Infantry, Gunner Charles Hughes, Royal Garrison Artillery, Private A. Smith and Driver James Pullen, killed by a shell 29 April 1918, all lived there.

There were other cottages in the vicinity including those in Rogers Lane and Duffield Lane, whose occupants included workers and servants of the Stoke Court Estate, ten of whom served in the war.

South Hill Cottages

Seven men from the six terraced dwellings known as South Hill Cottages in Rogers Lane served in the war and all survived. They were A. Bryant, C. Bryant, G. Bryant, John Dunton, Herbert Enstone, W. Overshott and J. Savin. Bill Overshott was wounded during fighting at Hill 60. He suffered, apart from a wound in his head, from the effects of gas poisoning, and from severe rheumatism contracted while lying out in a wet trench when wounded. He regained consciousness in Reading Hospital four days after his bullet wound at Ypres. He was under treatment there for two-and-a-half years. When he was demobilised after some four years' treatment the bullet was still somewhere in his body, and it was not removed until 1952, 38 years after the wound: by then it had worked down from the temple to below a shoulder blade.

61 *Bill Overshott.*

Sefton Park Cottages

62 *Sefton Park Cottages.*

In July 1915 the Parish Magazine printed this item: 'All the men of Sefton Park Cottages who can are serving their country either at home or abroad. It has been suggested that these houses should be renamed "Patriotic Terrace".'

Nine men volunteered from the eight cottages. They were Hugh Brown, Arthur Cull, Charles Gedge, Frank, Sidney and Walter Measday, Henry Mortlock, Lionel Tansley and Richard Thompson. Three of them, Sidney and Walter Measday and Arthur Cull, lost their lives. Mrs Wakefield, whose husband Major Charles Wakefield died in 1920 in the former German East Africa, lived in 8, Sefton Park Cottages.

H. Mortlock, a telegraphist in the Royal Navy, wrote home in February 1919 from the Sea of Marmora that he had received his Christmas parcel at Izmir in Turkey on 6 January 1919. He wrote that the Bolshevists were creating disturbances in the Black Sea ports, so they were remaining out there 'to protect our interests'.

Stoke House

Stoke House, Stoke Green, was built in 1821 as a private house. It became a school in the middle of the 19th century and became Stoke House in 1874 when the school founded in Clifton moved to Stoke Poges. The Reverend John St John

63 *Stoke House.*

64 *Stoke House Cricket Field.*

65 *Stoke Green.*

Parry was the headmaster of this preparatory school for Eton. It flourished under Parry's son Edward. Edward Parry was prominent in local affairs as a churchwarden, district councillor and chairman of the Parish Council. Many of the village boys, later to serve in the war, played cricket against the Stoke House boys. Some of the villagers were to serve under Lieutenant Martin Bowen in the Oxford and Bucks Light Infantry. Two of Parry's sons were officers as were many of the school's old boys. Stoke House moved to Seaford, probably in 1913. In 1965 it amalgamated with Brunswick School in East Grinstead, West Sussex, where one of its four houses is called Parry House.

66 *The* Red Lion *is still a popular public house in Stoke Green.*

67 *Red Lion Cottages is where the estate workers lived.*

68 *Stoke Park Mansion.*

Stoke Green

Twenty-five men from Stoke Green served, including Richard Howard-Vyse. Most of them worked on the Howard-Vyse Estate and included two of the Vallis family from the *Red Lion*. Two of the estate workers gave their lives, Frederick King and Harry Hammond, and two Werrell sisters from Stoke Green Farm – Winifred, who married Robert Cowell, and Edith, who married Charles Johnson – lost the husbands they met during the war. Sergeant Harry Newns who married into the Didcock family of Stoke Green also lost his life.

Stoke Park Estate

Twenty men from Stoke Park served in various regiments and the Royal Navy; most worked on the golf course. Three lost their lives, William Mayne, Edwin Shepherd, whose father worked on the golf course, and Harold Skues.

69 *Stoke Park Mansion Gardens.*

70 *Stoke Common.*

71 *Private G.Baylis, Oxford and Bucks Light Infantry, taken prisoner on 21 March 1918, and Able Seaman H.Harding, Royal Navy, both lived in Vine Cottages. These cottages stood where the entrance to Vine Road is now located.*

72 *Able Seaman Henry Harding.*

Men also came from other parts of the parish including Stoke Common, Farnham Road, Hockley Hole and Holly Bush Hill.

Twenty-four men were from Farnham Road, including Jardine Cottages, known now as Templewood Lane. They included Captain George Walmsley and his brother Lieutenant Alan Walmsley, MC, from Rough Hey. Arthur Bunby, Herbert Albrow and Arthur Plumridge, who lost their lives, were all from Farnham Road. A further 15 men were from Stoke Common, including Ralph Stahr, who was badly wounded and died at Loos, and Alfred Albrow who died in 1920.

PART TWO

Chapter Seven

The Men Who Gave Their Lives

'Each day, for the next four years and more, men and women throughout Europe would dread the arrival of a telegram announcing that they had lost a son, a brother or a husband. Every day those who perused the casuality lists knew that they might find a relative, or friend or a loved one.'

Martin Gilbert, *First World War*

Alfred Albrow – An Addition to the Roll of Honour

Jeremiah Albrow, by trade a paper-hanger, was born in Lowestoft. He moved to London and married Elisa and they had three sons. Two of them, Herbert and Alfred, were born in St Pancras, London, in 1879 and 1881. The youngest, Edmund, was born after his parents moved to Stoke Poges.

In 1894 Jeremiah was elected to the newly created Stoke Poges Parish Council. His son Herbert followed in his father's footsteps and became a paper-hanger and Alfred a painter and decorator.

The first to join up was the youngest son, Edmund, in May 1916. He served in the 20th County of London Regiment, and survived the war only to be killed after it in a cycling accident on the Bath Road, Slough.

Alfred Gladstone Albrow joined the Bedfordshire Regiment in October 1916, having married Louisa Gilder in 1912. They had three children, George William born in 1914, a daughter Gladys born the following year and a second daughter Marjorie.

Alfred later transferred to the Labour Corps. He was discharged from the army but is recorded on the Commonwealth War Graves Commission Debt of Honour Register. He died as a result of his wounds, at the aged of 39, on 11 February 1920 at his home 'The Cottage', Stoke Common, Stoke Poges.

73 *Alfred Albrow with his wife Louisa and their children Gladys Rosina, George William and Marjorie Catherine.*

He is not recorded on the Memorial Tablet in St Giles' Church because it had been erected before he died. The Parish Magazine of March 1920 records the death of three ex-servicemen who all died within a few weeks of each other, and who lived near each other: Alfred Albrow, Henry Holdship and Archibald Tyson. It stated:

The Roll of Honour
To our Roll must be added the names of the following soldiers, all from Farnham Road, who came back broken in health from the war, died in consequence of it. We commend them to the love and mercy of our God.
Archibald McK Tyson
Henry Holdship
Alfred Gladstone Albrow

Alfred Albrow is buried in Stoke Poges Churchyard with his wife Louisa who died on 13 July 1961.

Herbert Albrow – Died in Palestine

Herbert Edward, the eldest of Jeremiah and Eliza Albrow's three sons, joined the army in October 1916, having married Elizabeth Piner in 1908. They had six children, including twins, one of whom died in infancy.

Herbert originally enlisted in the Army Service Corps and was employed as a motor transport driver. Sometime late in 1916 or early in 1917 he was transferred to an infantry-training unit. The costly Battle of the Somme had finally drawn to a close in November 1916 leaving the infantry short of men. This was probably the reason the War Office was transferring men from the Army Service Corps to the infantry.

After training Herbert was posted, with a draft of 124 men, to 1/4th Battalion, Duke of Cornwall's Light Infantry on 4 April 1917. A month later his unit set sail for Alexandria but his ship was torpedoed. A number of 1/4th Duke of Cornwall casualties were incurred at sea on 4 May 1917, the same day that the Anchor Line ship RMS *Transylvania* was torpedoed by *U 63* in the Gulf of Genoa, close to Cape Valda. It seems probable that this was Herbert Albrow's ship.

Two Japanese destroyers, *Matsu* and *Sakaki*, were escorting the *Transylvania*. After the first torpedo struck, the *Matsu* started to offload passengers from the stricken ship leaving the *Sakaki* to deal with the U-boat. However, the *Transylvania* was struck by a second torpedo and sank rapidly, some three to four miles off shore.

Of the 3,060 crew and troops, 414 lost their lives. The survivors were put ashore at Savona and after rest were transported by rail back to Marseille. Herbert finally reached the Middle East to join his battalion on 28 June 1917.

He received his 1917 Christmas parcel and wrote home:

> It reached me where we are miles away from any town, and we have not seen a place to buy anything since July. I think it would open the eyes of everyone in Stoke if they could see how the natives live here. Apparently they have not changed for generations.

The War Diary of the 1/4th Battalion of the Duke of Cornwall's Light Infantry records that it was in action at Rafat, Palestine, on 27 April 1918, when Herbert Albrow was killed:

> At 0200 a raid was made on the Ridge coy. (B) under cover of a bombardment, but the raiders were easily driven off. At the same time a very heavy trench mortar bombardment of the village took place, together with a barrage of 4.2in. and 77mm shells on the southern slope of wadi LEHHAM. Immediately after the bombardment a small party of the enemy attacked the village and obtained a footing at the N.W. corner, from which they were driven out. Everything was quiet again by 0345.

In this action one officer and seven other ranks were killed and died of wounds, with 21 wounded and two missing. B Battery of the 37th Royal Field Artillery fired 320 rounds in support but a considerable number of these were duds.

The Parish Magazine reported his death:

> Private H.E. Albrow, M.T., we regret to learn, was killed in action on April 27th, leaving a widow and six children, who have our deepest sympathy. He started for the east over a year ago, and his ship was torpedoed. After a rest in France he again embarked and has been in the east ever since. Private Albrow lived at 16, Farnham Road, carrying on the business of house decorator.

Herbert Albrow was buried in Ramleh War Cemetery, Israel, grave reference N.48. He was 39 years of age.

Robert Alsford – The Last Stoke Poges Man to be Killed

Robert Thomas Alsford was born in Langley in 1890, the son of Frederick and Mary Alsford, and one of their eight children. Frederick had his own brick making business in George Green.

Robert, who lived in Rex Cottages, Wexham Street, enlisted in September 1914 in the Middlesex Regiment, known as the Duke of Cambridge's Own.

Robert Alsford died on Monday 4 November 1918, with the rank of corporal according to the Parish Magazine, just seven days before the armistice. He was the last Stoke Poges man to be killed in action and on the same day that the poet Wilfred Owen lost his life. The War Diary of the 13th Battalion, in which Robert was serving in C company, records that on the previous day, 3 November:

> During the afternoon patrols having found that the enemy had retired the line was advanced and at dusk was established on the line JENLAIN (exclusive) VILLERS POL (exclusive). A and D coys. in front line. C and B in support. C Coy. having crossed from S of the LARHONELLE river.

And for the next day, 4 November, when Robert was killed:

> The remaining Battns of the brigade passed through this Battn at 06.30 and drove the enemy over the AUNELLE River. This being effected the 13th Mx concentrated towards the left near LE CORON and advanced through WARGNIES LE GRAND, during the afternoon. A line was established E of that village, considerable opposition being experienced from machine guns …

74 *The Post Office in Wexham.*

Robert Alsford, who was unmarried, died at the age of 29, having served throughout the war until its final days. He is buried in Cross Roads Cemetery, Nord, France, grave reference IV.D.10. He is commemorated on both the Stoke Poges and George Green Memorials. His older brother William Henry died of his wounds on 10 January 1920, aged 36, and is buried in the north-east corner of Langley Marish (St Mary) Churchyard.

John Bateman – The *Remindo* Sunk on a Secret Mission

Levi John Bateman, born and educated in Stoke Poges, joined the Royal Navy as a 15-year-old in 1912. The Bateman family was well known locally. John's uncle was William Bateman, a long serving local bell ringer who died in 1953 aged 83. His daughter, John's cousin, was Gladys who married Arthur Barker and continued the bell ringing tradition of the family until she died in 1998 aged 98.

75 *HMS* Queen Elizabeth *under fire from the Turkish batteries at the entrance to the Dardanelles, 18 March 1915, during the ill-fated attempt to force the Narrows of Chanak. Jack Bateman in his letter home describes this action. (Photograph: Liddle Centre for World War I.)*

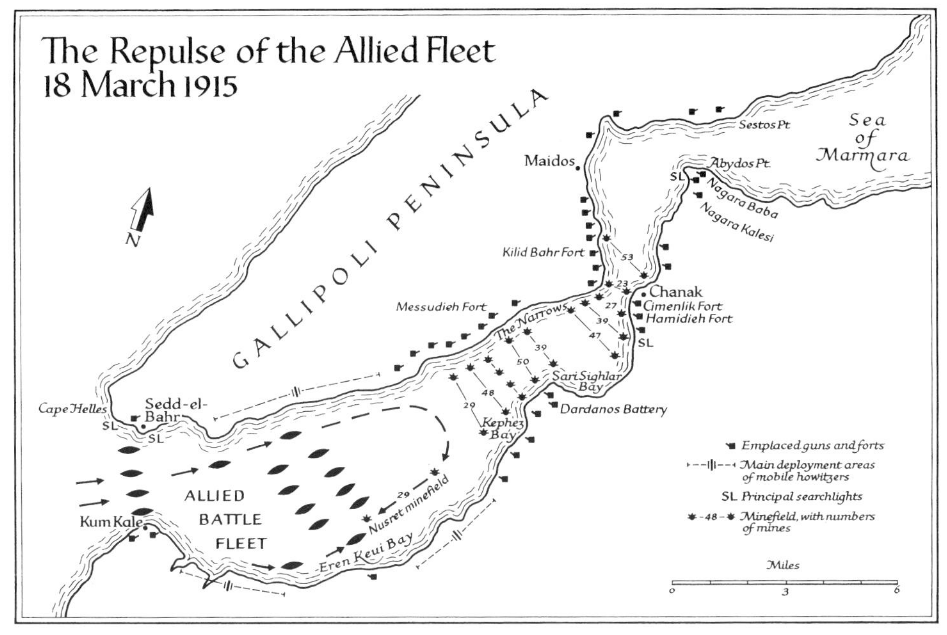

76 *Map of the naval attack of 18 March 1915 showing the points of farthest penetration, reproduced by kind permission of Sir Martin Gilbert, CBE.,D.Litt.*

On joining the Navy, Jack, as he was known, was described as being 5ft 1in high, chest 32 inches, brown hair, grey eyes, fair complexion and his occupation was telegraph boy.

He became a signal boy and served on various ships, joining HMS *Queen Elizabeth* in December 1914, being promoted to assistant signalman and then signalman, and serving on this ship until February 1917.

The *Queen Elizabeth* was completed in January 1915 just after John joined it. It was the first battleship designed to burn oil fuel alone, was the first to mount 15-inch guns and had a speed of 25 knots. Ships in this class were probably the most successful battleships ever built.

HMS *Queen Elizabeth* sailed for the Dardanelles at the end of January 1915 and the Parish Magazine published a letter from John Bateman in May 1915:

> We get our mail fairly regularly; usually a week's at a time. We left Portsmouth after dark on January 29th; we went into Portland and got oiled, left there and arrived at Gibraltar, after a rough voyage, on the 5th February, stayed there, going out occasionally for firing, till the 13th, when we left for an unknown destination eastwards. We passed Malta on 17th and proceeded direct to the Dardanelles, where we arrived on 19th. Since then, weather permitting, we have bombarded every day. We are flagship. We made a dash about a week ago up to the Narrows and unfortunately lost the French ship *Bouvet* and the English *Irresistible* and *Ocean* – (the *Bouvet* lost all her hands and the *Ocean* and *Irresistible* a few) – with several others damaged. We ourselves were lucky, having one large hole in the funnel and one large one in the upper deck, but nothing serious and no casualties at all.

> On the whole we were very successful and we are believed to have put their great Forts out of action. The Narrows is the hardest place we shall find, the forts, which are reckoned to be impregnable, are not much use against our 15-inch guns, which throw a projectile weighing a ton. You ought to see them drop! They don't half move something – especially Turks. The Turks have got aeroplanes on the go here now trying to drop bombs, but they only make a target for our high-angle guns. We have got some daring airmen out here too, including the German's '£1,000 dead or alive' airman. Some of the forts are manned entirely by Germans.
>
> The Turks have three different ways of laying mines in the Dardanelles. (1) Anchored mines, exploded when struck (2) floating mines, exploded when struck or when they strike themselves, and (3) observation mines, exploded by electricity from shore. They have also fixed torpedo tubes, and these must be destroyed from shore, and troops are required for that job. So it will be slow but sure. We have only mines and 'subs' to fear here. It was mines that sank the others. I hope it will be our job to sink the *Goeben* later on.
>
> I went shore today to stretch my legs, and I saw oxen ploughing in the fields and donkeys with baskets on, just like you read about in the Bible. I have written to Mr Pridden, gunner (HMS *Implacable*). He was almost alongside us yesterday (25th). It is a great sport out here, and you must not worry at all, because we are quite happy out here. I have had some Turkish delight! Remember me to all, and keep smiling. I am quite well, and we are giving the Turks what they asked for.

In February 1917 John transferred to another ship, although its name was not disclosed in the Parish Magazine. It was the *Renown*, completed in 1916, and it served with the First Battle-Cruiser Squadron until the end of the war. (*Renown* brought Winston Churchill back from the Quebec Conference in 1943 and was broken up in 1947.)

Sometime before February 1918, John Bateman volunteered for 'Secret Service' on board the 'fish hydrophone trawler' *Remindo*. His mother received a letter, dated 7 February 1918, from the Admiralty, that read:

> It is my painful duty to inform you that telegraphic information has been received in this Department to the effect that H.M. Trawler *Remindo* was sunk by an explosion on the 2nd instant. No survivors have been reported, and in these circumstances it is deeply regretted that Levi John Bateman, Signalman, Official No. J 20560, who was serving on board, must be regarded as having lost his life.

There were three officers and 17 ratings on board. No information is available as to the *Remindo*'s mission or the cause of the explosion. The Admiralty listed the cause of death as drowned at sea, killed by enemy action.

The report in the Parish Magazine assumed that the *Remindo* had been torpedoed. It recalled that John Bateman, who had recently been on leave and singing heartily in the church, was 'the sweetest boy-singer we ever had in the choir'.

John Bateman was 21 when he died on 2 February 1918 and is commemorated on the Portsmouth Naval Memorial, panel number 29.

Arthur James Birch – 64th Company, Machine Gun Corps

James and Ellen Birch had three sons who served in the army and two of them did not return. William Joseph was born in 1889, Arthur James in 1890 and Albert in 1897. Like his brothers, Arthur was born in Stoke Poges and was called up in February 1916. Private Arthur Birch went to France in July of that year and was killed on the Somme, on Saturday, 16 September 1916, aged 26.

Arthur worked first at Sefton Park and then at Wyfold Court, probably as a gardener. The Parish Magazine of November 1916 published this extract from a letter his mother received from the officer commanding his section:

> He was struck by a shell and died at once, suffering no pain at all. I found him to be a sound and reliable man and deplore his loss. He died nobly doing his duty.

The 64th Company, Machine Gun Corps, 21st Battalion Diary, records that on 16 September 1916, at 2.30 a.m., the 64th Company marched from Pommier Redoubt Camp to take part in an attack on enemy trenches near Flers.

Arthur Birch was 26 and his body was not recovered. He is commemorated on Thiepval Memorial, Somme, panel number pier and face 5C and 12C.

77 *Mrs Ellen Birch, mother of Arthur and William, at the door of their house on Bells Hill.*

William Joseph Birch – A Casualty of Shelling

William Joseph Birch was the eldest of the three Birch brothers who served in the war. He was 28 when he died of wounds on 15 August 1917.

William's younger brother Albert, who survived the war, recalled that his father was gardener and coachman to Mr Williams of 'Uplands' in Rogers Lane.* The family lived on Bells Hill. William, who was also a gardener, married Louisa Boon at St Peter's Church, Burnham, in November 1915 before enlisting. They lived at Yew Tree Cottages, Farnham Common.

William, who was born in Stoke Poges, served in the 1/4th Battalion of the Oxford and Bucks Light Infantry. Albert Birch recalled visiting his brother's grave in Etaples Military Cemetery when he was there during his military service. Etaples had a number of military hospitals.

On 5 August 1917 the 1/4th Battalion moved up to the front line in the Ypres Salient along the Steenbeck and suffered several casualties while taking over. The Regimental Record lists the dispositions of the four companies on 7 August and states that continuous shelling caused many further casualties. The heavy

---

* Birch, Albert, 'The Memories of Albert Birch', *Stoke Poges Parish Newsletter*, No. 31 August 1974.

78 *William Joseph Birch.*

shelling continued the next day with further casualties until the battalion was relieved at night. During these three days three officers and 18 men were killed, two officers and 58 men wounded, with four men missing.

The battalion spent the following week in training until returning to the front line late in the evening of 15 August. This suggests that Private William Birch was probably wounded during the three days 5 to 7 August in the Battle of Passchendaele and subsequently evacuated to one of the base hospitals at Etaples, near Boulogne.

William Joseph Birch is buried in Etaples Military Cemetery, Pas de Calais, grave reference XXll.P.19. He is commemorated on the Burnham War Memorial, St Mary's Church, Hedgerley, as well as in St Giles' Church, Stoke Poges.

Harold Bowen – Returned from Canada

Harold Thomas Bowen was born on 9 July 1890. His family lived in Appletons, Grays Park Road, where Bawn House now stands. He was the son of John Bowen, a solicitor, and Christina, his wife. They had two other sons, Martin, who was six years younger than Harold and who was also killed in the First World War. The third son, Lieut-Commander D. Bowen, who was at Jutland, survived the War.

Harold, like his brother, was educated at Rossall School, Lancashire. He left home for Canada when very young where he was working to raise enough money to buy a fruit farm. He had served for three years in the British Columbia Horse, a militia unit, and was a corporal when war broke out. On 8 December 1914 he enlisted at Victoria, British Columbia, in the 2nd Canadian Mounted Rifles (formerly the British Columbia Horse) for service in the Canadian Overseas Expeditionary Force. He was single, aged 24, and gave his occupation as rancher. His attestation papers disclose that he was tall, 6ft 2½ in, with brown eyes and hair, dark complexion and a chest measurement fully expanded of 38 inches.

Harold achieved fairly rapid promotion, sergeant in April 1915 and quartermaster-sergeant in September 1915 when he disembarked in France with the 8th Infantry Brigade, 3rd Canadian Division. In September 1916 he was wounded on the Somme when a bullet apparently went through his helmet and traced its way along the top of his head.

In July 1917, he was promoted to temporary lieutenant. Returning to the front in December 1917, he was wounded by a shell in the trenches late in the evening of 1 January 1918. Lieut Bowen was taken to Number 7 Casualty Clearing Station and died at 7.45 a.m. the next day. He only lived a few hours and never regained consciousness.

His obituary in the parish magazine recorded:

> After taking a commission he went back to the front … notwithstanding the fact that, owing to the severity of a previous wound, he could have stayed at home and had a softer job. But his grit and determination to serve his country again urged him on, and he refused to stay behind. All honour to such deliberate self-sacrifice.

A very well attended service was held in St Giles' Church on Saturday 12 January 1918, in memory of the two Bowen brothers. At this service the names of all from the village who had fallen were also read out.

Harold Bowen is buried in Mazingarbe Communal Cemetery Extension, Pas de Calais, grave reference III.A.10. In September 1918 his father, John Evan Bowen, moved from Stoke Poges to Bexhill-on-Sea. He died at the age of 70 and was buried in St Giles' Churchyard in May 1926.

Martin Bowen, MC – The Capture of Tombois Farm

Martin Bowen was Harold Bowen's younger brother. He was educated at Stoke House (Parry's Prep School in Stoke Green) and Rossall School where he was in the shooting VIII, representing the school for two years at Bisley. He had just completed his last term when war broke out. He was commissioned in the Oxford and Bucks Light Infantry and went to France in April 1915.

On 23 August 1916 the 1/1st Battalion moved into the trenches between Thiepval and Ovilliers on the Somme. They carried out an attack on the enemy's forward positions that same day at 15.05 after a five-minute artillery bombardment. Unfortunately the bombardment fell short and was immediately followed by an enemy barrage with the result that there were heavy casualties making progress impossible. No real gain resulted from this action. Two officers and 24 other ranks were killed and two officers, including Lieut Martin Bowen, and 71 other ranks were wounded.

After hospitalisation Lieut Bowen returned to the front. The period February to April 1917 saw the German retirement from the Somme. During this time there were several minor operations against enemy posts forward of the Hindenburg Line.

On 16 and 17 April he took part in an operation to capture Tombois Farm and a ridge due east of the farm and close to the Hindenburg Line.

This operation was carried out in extremely unfavourable weather conditions for an attack at night over open country with few landmarks. It was

79 *The grave of Martin Bowen.*

pitch-black, with pouring rain and a gale blowing in the direction of the enemy. On the right was C Company with B Company led by Bowen on the left and D Company in echelon behind. The Parish Magazine later reported that there were several Stoke men in B company.

Capt. P.L. Wright in his book, *The First Buckinghamshire Battalion 1914-19*, gives this account of the action:

80 *Captain Martin Bowen, MC.*

> At 11.46 p.m. the enemy opened with machine-gun and rifle fire, and sent up a great number of lights from the farm and the trenches on either side of it. They also put down a moderate barrage well behind our attack, mostly on the outskirts of Lempire and on Sart Farm. All companies encountered a thick belt of wire in front of the enemy positions, which were strongly held, C and D Companies both being held up by this wire, which it was impossible to negotiate in face of the heavy enemy fire. All D Company's officers had become casualties, and at 12.30 a.m. Captain Hales decided to withdraw both companies to Sart Farm, and to reform them there for another attack.
>
> Meanwhile B Company, on the left, had attracted rather less rifle and machine-gun fire than the other two companies, and had succeeded in getting through a thinner belt of wire and penetrating the enemy trenches at a point just north of where the trench crossed the road.
>
> In consequence of the failure of the two right companies, and in view of the fact that at that time no news had been received at Battalion Headquarters of the success of B Company's attack, three platoons of the support company (1/5th Battalion Gloucestershire Regiment) were ordered to advance on the farm, one platoon each side of the road and one in close support, in order to ascertain the situation as regards B Company and, if necessary, to attack. They arrived at the farm to find B Company in possession, but the enemy still holding out in the orchard south of the farm. Our men were finding considerable difficulty in clearing the orchard owing to the fire of the other two companies who had been held up.
>
> By 3 a.m., however, both farm and orchard were clear, and a counter-attack, launched by the enemy down the road, was successfully broken by B Company.

Martin Bowen, subsequently promoted to captain, was awarded the Military Cross for his part in the capture of Tombois Farm. The official report stated 'He led his Company in the most gallant manner, and in spite of very difficult conditions succeeded in gaining his objective. He set a fine example to his men.'

Martin Bowen was shot by a sniper on 3 October during the third Battle of Ypres, and died on 10 October 1917. He was buried on the hillside above Wimereux in Wimereux Communal Cemetery, grave reference IV.N.1. which is five kilometres north of Boulogne. The Canadian Lieut-Colonel John McCrae, author of the poem 'In Flanders Fields', is also buried in this cemetery.

His housemaster at Rossall, Mr Furneaux, wrote of him in his obituary that Martin Bowen 'was gifted with a very charming natural character, full of kindliness and thoughtfulness for others. If his manner was a little rugged and abrupt, it was part of his downright sincerity. Into every subject which he took up he threw himself with ardour and thoroughness, and this quality stood him in good stead when he obeyed the call to arms in 1914.'

Arthur George Bunby – The Confusion of a Gas Attack

Arthur George Bunby came from an old Stoke Poges family. His grandfather John Thomas Bunby had been landlord of the *Dog and Pot* and Edward, his father, landlord of the *Oddfellows Arms*, now known as Winterclyde. By the outbreak of war, Arthur was married to Katie who, after he was killed, moved to Rickmansworth. His parents lived at 20 Farnham Road, now known as Templewood Lane.

Arthur was an early volunteer who joined the 1st Battalion of the Bedfordshire Regiment. It was during the second battle of Ypres that Arthur fell victim to an enemy gas attack. The Germans used chlorine gas twice in April 1915, the first time ever gas was used, and in May there were four more such attacks on the Ypres Salient.

5.5.15 Near Hill 60

At a little after 8 a.m. enemy attacked with asphyxiating gas laid on from two points opposite our trenches. Battn stuck to its trenches, though a few men killed by gas & all were badly affected. Troops on right however were driven out of trenches, & enemy captured Hill 60 & trenches on our immediate right. Our left trenches were then attacked but drove back enemy: our right trenches were attacked all day with bombs, rifles & machine guns. Desperate fight all day enemy & selves in same trench, both sides using handgrenades freely. Enemy eventually worked round our right flank & enfiladed our right, but men gallantly maintained their position. A Battery of our own artillery

81 *Extract from the War Diary of the 1st Battalion, Bedfordshire Regiment, describing the gas attack on 5 May 1915.*

Arthur Bunby died on 5 May 1915 in a gas attack. Another soldier of the 2nd Battalion of the Bedfordshires, Private W.A. Quinton, has left a vivid description of a gas attack a few days earlier, which he survived. They had drawn their flannel belts from their haversacks, soaked them in water and tied them round their mouths and noses. He continued:

> We caught our first whiff of it. No words of mine can ever describe my feelings as we inhaled the first mouthful. We choked, spit, and coughed, my lungs felt as though they were burnt out, and were going to burst. Red hot needles were being thrust into my eyes. --- The first impulse was to run. --- We had just seen men running to certain death, and knew it, rather than stay and be choked into a slow and agonising death. It was one of those occasions when you do not know what you are doing. The man who stayed was no braver than the man who ran away. We crouched there, terrified --- stupefied. We lay with our noses in the mud, fighting for breath.*

Arthur Bunby's experience of a similar gas attack came on 5 May, south of Ypres. The War Diary of the 1st Battalion of the Bedfordshire Regiment records the event:

> At a little after 8 a.m. enemy attacked with asphyxiating gas laid† on from two points opposite our trenches. Battalion stuck to the trenches though a few men were killed by gas and all were badly affected. Troops on the right however were driven out of the trenches, and enemy captured Hill 60 and trenches on our immediate right. Our left trenches were then attacked but drove back enemy: our right trenches were attacked all day with bombs, rifles and machine guns. Desperate fight all day enemy and selves in same trench, both sides using hand grenades freely.
>
> Enemy eventually worked round our right flank and enfiladed‡ our right, but men gallantly maintained their position. A Battery of our own artillery spent the whole day firing into our right trenches, causing many casualties but in spite of everything right trenches held out. Lt. Whittemore alone claims over 50 Germans to his own rifle, and he was seen by Artillery Observing Officer to shoot seven Germans in a couple of minutes.
>
> Our casualties in right trenches were heavy. Lt. Hopkins killed, Capt. Gledstones and Lt. Whittemore wounded.
>
> Attack made by 13th Inf. Bt. to recapture Hill 60 and re-establish line not successful.
>
> (Capt. Gledstones died of wounds).

It is small wonder in the confusion of the battle, surrounded by such uncertainty, that Private Arthur Bunby was reported as wounded and missing,

---

* Memoirs of Private W.A.Quinton, 2nd Battalion, Bedfordshire Regiment, held in the Department of Documents at the Imperial War Museum, reference 79/35/1.

† In the early gas attacks the gas was released from cylinders but later was delivered by artillery shells as well.

‡ enfiladed – to be in a position to rake with shot through the whole length of a line.

leaving his family with the hope he might be a prisoner. The Parish Magazine in reporting this news assured its readers 'from recent accounts it would seem that our prisoners in Germany are treated better now than was the case earlier in the war.' It was left to Corporal Monks, a comrade, to write from hospital, where he was recovering from the effects of the gas attack, to inform Mrs Bunby there was little hope of him being still alive.

Arthur George Bunby was 29 years of age and his body was not recovered. He is commemorated on the Ypres (Menin Gate) Memorial, panels 31 and 33. His two brothers survived the war.

82 *The grave of Eric Clark in St Giles' Churchyard.*

Eric Clark – A 17-Year-old Victim of the Influenza Epidemic

Eric Allison Clark was the youngest from Stoke Poges to die and he had the shortest length of service. He was not yet 18, when he died on 20 October 1918 in Blandford Military Hospital, a fortnight after volunteering for service as a draughtsman in the Royal Air Force. He died of influenza in the great pandemic that claimed the lives of 150,000 Britons.

Eric was the son of John and Jessie Clark who lived at Stoke Wood Cottage, Stoke Common. John was a silver engraver and he passed his gifts of draughtsmanship on to his son. They had both been responsible for the inscribed lists of men serving in the war, which had been displayed in the St Giles' Church and the Mission Room in Templewood Lane.

Eric, who was in the local scout troop, went to Stoke Poges School and Slough Secondary School after which he joined the drawing office at Messrs Peters. He is buried in St Giles' Churchyard, south of the main path, past the first lych-gate.

Reginald Clifton – Killed in an Advance on the Somme

Reginald Horace Clifton was the youngest of the three sons of William and Agnes Clifton. Born in 1898 and educated at Marlborough, he enlisted as a private in the RAMC in December 1915, not being old enough to join a regiment.

He transferred to the 1/6th Battalion of the Manchester Regiment in 1916:

> This Battalion was involved in an advance on the Somme on 21st August 1918 which proved to be only partially successful. On that day the Battalion lost 1 officer wounded, 15 other ranks killed and 24 other ranks wounded. That was the price paid for the limited amount of ground gained, some 50 prisoners captured and 6 light machine guns taken. Pte Clifton, aged 20, was one of those killed ...*

---

* Harvey, Trevor, 'If I should die ...', *Stoke Poges Parish Newsletter*, No.73, December 1984.

The Parish Magazine of October 1918 contained a short obituary: -

> In 1916 he transferred into the 1/6th Manchesters, and the following January joined their Division in Egypt, and in March 1917, they arrived in France. Reggie Clifton became 'runner' to his Sergeant and afterwards to his Captain, both of whom with many others admired his great pluck and daring ...

Reginald Clifton is buried in Queen's Cemetery, Bucquoy, Pas de Calais, grave reference II.D.7. A mounted stained glass window in the entrance to St Andrew's Church, Rogers Lane, Stoke Poges also commemorates him and his brother. This originally formed part of a window in St Wilfred's Chapel in Chapel Lane, Stoke Poges, which was demolished in 1973.

W.G.T. Clifton – RFC – A Victim of the Richthofen Circus

William Gerard Talbot Clifton was one of two brothers who were both killed in the war.

Talbot Clifton volunteered at the outbreak of war and signed on as a trooper in the 1/1st City of London Yeomanry known as the Rough Riders. Yeomanry Regiments were cavalry regiments made up of part-time soldiers, territorials, who served dismounted. The first winter of the war was spent guarding the East Coast. It was at Gallipoli that he took part in the charge of the Yeomanry on foot, on 21 October 1915, to take Chocolate Hill, where he was wounded in the right arm and sent back to England.*

In November 1915, Talbot was commissioned into the 3rd Battalion of the Oxford and Bucks Light Infantry and was sent to France. On 30 December 1916 he was selected for the Royal Flying Corps and joined 11 Squadron as an observer. Three months later, in March 1917, he was mortally wounded. The Parish Magazine reported:

> On 31st March, when acting as an observer over German lines, his machine was brought down near the village of Bailleul. The pilot wounded and a prisoner, wrote, 'I am sorry my observer was badly wounded. My machine was shot to blazes and I think I had the luck in bringing the machine down to the ground without crashing.' Since then there has been silence until the last sad news came in.

2nd Lieut Clifton was taken prisoner, but died the same day, aged 23, in the Field Hospital at Corbehem.

> Records have not survived to show how many times Lieut. Clifton flew but it is possible to piece together the details of his last flight. No.11 Squadron was a reconnaissance unit flying FE2b's, a two-seater biplane with its engine mounted to face the rear in order that the observer in the front cockpit had the widest field of vision and to provide the maximum field of fire for the two Lewis guns he manned. At 6.20 a.m.

* The City of London Yeomanry landed in Gallipoli with strength of 17 officers and 315 other ranks and when it left the Peninsula, 2 November 1915, it had been reduced to five officers and 46 other ranks. See Westlake, Ray, *British Regiments at Gallipoli* (1996), pp. 263/4.

on 31st March 1916, 6 FE2b's of 11 Squadron took off to rendezvous with 4 Nieuport fighters of 60 Squadron who were to act as escorts. During the patrol over enemy territory the formation was attacked.

In a letter to *Popular Flying* published in April 1934, the pilot of FE2b No.7691 Lieut. L.A. Strange explained, 'I was shot down by Lieut. Wolff of the Richthofen Circus on the morning of 31st March 1917 at Gavrelle, I regret to say that the first burst from Wolff's guns mortally wounded my observer, Lieut. Clifton, and almost immediately afterwards my engine cut out owing to the tank being riddled with bullets. It was necessary to tip the machine up on her nose in order to lift Lieut. Clifton out.' Lieut. Strange, himself wounded, was taken prisoner. A letter he wrote whilst a prisoner to his father was the evidence accepted of William Clifton's death.*

83 *Memorial to the Clifton brothers in St Andrew's Church, Stoke Poges. Originally in St Wilfred's Chapel in Chapel Lane, it was transferred to the new church in 1972 after the chapel was demolished.*

William Gerard Talbot Clifton is buried in Corbehem Communal Cemetery, a village to the south-west of Douai, Pas de Calais, France. The son of William and Agnes Clifton of The Bungalow, Stoke Poges, his parents suffered the tragedy of also losing another son Reginald (*see* pp. 83-4).

George Clinch – Died of Dysentery at Gaza

George Clinch was born in Duckington, Oxfordshire. We find him in the 1901 census, at the age of 20, a carpenter living as a lodger in Eltham, London. His father John Clinch died and his mother Sarah remarried and is listed as Mrs S.Wells. George's connection with Stoke Poges was forged when he married Emily Davis of Hockley Hole.

George enlisted in the 13th Kensington Battalion of the London Regiment. He served over two years in Salonika, for a long spell in Egypt, and finally in Palestine where he died of dysentery. He left a widow and three children. When he died 28 October 1918 he was 40 years of age.

* Harvey, Trevor, 'If I should die ...', *Stoke Poges Parish Newsletter*, No.73, December 1984.

84 *Ibrahim Jeradeh, the Palestinian gardener who tends the Gaza War Cemetery. (Photograph: courtesy Telegraph Group, photographer Debbie Hill.)*

The Chaplain wrote:

> You will like to know that on October 27th, the Sunday, we were able to have a holy Communion Service in the ward, and he joined in most gladly. He laid listening and quietly followed the prayers and received the Holy Communion. We sang hymns 160 and 332, and afterwards he told me he had been very glad of it all. Next morning he passed away.

The Matron of the Hospital also wrote to Mrs Clinch:

> He put up such a brave fight for it, never complaining, but bore his troubles so bravely and patiently and always grateful. The message he told me to send was 'Send my love to the wife and children'.

Private George Clinch is buried in Gaza War Cemetery, Israel, grave reference XXVII.F.8. Ibrahim Jeradeh, a Palestinian gardener, tends this cemetery. He succeeded his father, Rabia, as head gardener, and in 2001 he said that after 40 years' service he will pass on the duty to his son Issam Ibrahim. He was awarded the MBE in 1994 for his dedicated care of the cemetery over such a long time.

Tom Collison – Died as a Result of Shelling

Tom Charles Collison was born on 6 January 1885 at the *Stag*, Wexham Street, Stoke Poges, where his grandparents were the landlords. In 1887 his mother Amelia married William Banister and Tom grew up as part of the Banister family, having at the time of the 1901 census four half-brothers, John born 1889, Arthur born 1891, Herbert born 1895 and Wilfred born 1900. Tom left school and became a stable boy.

He married Lucy and by the end of the war she was living in Sheldon Road, Paddington, with their son Tommy. Tom Collison's name was not on the initial list of Stoke Poges men killed in the war, published in the Parish Magazine, but it was added to the revised list. However, and unfortunately, it was mis-spelt on the Memorial Tablet where it is recorded as Collinson. This is doubly unfortunate since young Tommy is recorded on a list as having subscribed towards the cost of the Memorial.

Tom Collison served in the Army Service Corps, Mechanical Transport, and was attached to 'G' Special Company of the Royal Engineers. This unit's job was to fire projectiles containing gas at the enemy, operations that depended on the wind and which sometimes resulted in projectiles bursting on being fired and the drums bursting in the guns. The job was unpleasant and required safety precautions to be taken. A report of one operation, undertaken a month before Tom Collison died, is described in the War Diary of 'G' Special Company:

> 12.3.18 Purpose of operation to inflict losses on enemy holding the trench system SW of Queant to lower his morale and to interfere with any possible concentration of troops at this point. This sector of the front is thought to be held by B.I.R. which, according to our records, has never been subjected to a British gas attack.
>
> 362 projectiles fired.
>
> The wind being very light, the cloud hung over the targets for a long time and may have done considerable damage. A number of projectiles (about 68) burst on being fired and the drums burst in the guns; a not inconsiderable quantity of gas was thus freed in the surroundings of the batteries but the safety precautions were entirely adequate.

This type of activity invited enemy attack and the unit was subjected to enemy shelling. The War Diary for the company for Monday 29 April 1918, the day Tom Collison died, reads:

> CHOCQUES 29 .4.18 1 O.R. struck off strength, 2 O.Rs admitted to hospital (sick), evac to CCS & struck off strength. 1 O.R. admitted to hospital (sick). 2 O.Rs killed. 2 O.Rs died of wounds. 18 O.Rs wounded (shell). 3 O.Rs wounded remaining on duty. 3 O.Rs N.Y.D. Gas.

Private Tom Collison died as a result of the shelling, aged 33, and is buried in Chocques Military Cemetery, Pas de Calais, France, grave reference VI.A.11. His half-brothers all survived the war and one of them, Arthur Banister, who was an ambulance driver, told his son in later life that he had met Tom in France 'after the shelling'. Tom's son Tommy became an optician and founded Collison's Opticians.

Robert Cowell – Coldstream Guardsman

Robert Cowell came from Seaham, Durham. His father, Emanuel, was a colliery weighman but he must have died leaving Eliza, his widow, with seven children because she remarried in 1895 when Robert was only four years old. The 1901 census reveals that her second husband was James Dunn, a coal miner. Robert, then aged 10, had a step-brother as a result of this second marriage, William Dunn who was also a coal miner.

Robert enlisted in the Coldstream Guards at Seaham Harbour in September 1914. Shortly afterwards he went to France where he was wounded. He returned to France and was wounded a second time and gassed. His connection with Stoke Poges was established when, as a young guardsman from Windsor barracks, he met Winifred Marian Werrell of Stoke Green Farm and married her at St Giles' Church on 23 September 1916.

Guardsman Robert Cowell was wounded a third time 23 July 1918 on the Somme front. On the day he was wounded the Battalion War Diary records that his company was working on roads and tracks and transporting RE material by night. He is then listed as one of four men who were wounded. He was taken to the 3rd Canadian Stationary Hospital with a gunshot wound from which he died. Aged 27, he left a young widow and a son Robert Jack, who was born four months before his father died.

The officer commanding the Canadian Hospital wrote to Mrs Cowell:

> Everything possible was done to save his life, and he had all the care and attention that medical science and good nursing could give. He was unconscious and therefore relieved of much pain. He was buried with full military honours in the military cemetery.

The cemetery used for those who died in the Canadian Hospital was Gezaincourt Communal Cemetery Extension, Somme. Robert Cowell's grave reference is I.O.12. Winifred Marian Cowell's sister Edith Mabel Werrell married Charles Jones Johnson, a South African soldier, in October 1917. He was killed three months after his brother-in-law (*see* p. 106).

Arthur Cull – A Casualty of the Third Battle of Ypres

Arthur John Cull was born in Ilkley, Yorkshire, and at the time of the 1901 census, when aged 16, he was an apprentice engineer living with his family in Edmonton, London.

His address in the 1918 Absent Voters Register was given as Sefton Park Cottages. Arthur, who was married, joined the 1st Battalion of the Queen's Own (Royal West Kent Regiment), probably early in 1915.

Arthur lost his life on 26 October 1917 fighting in the Third Battle of Ypres. On that day his battalion took part in an attack by two divisions on both sides of the Menin Road towards Gheluvelt near Ypres. The 7th Division on the south of the road failed to capture a group of pillboxes. The Queen's Own 1st Battalion War Diary recorded:

> At 8 am bodies of troops of the 7th Div. retreated across the Bt. front and these were collected as far as possible and with LT D.H. LEWIS BARNED were sent to hold a line of posts as near to the original front line as possible. C Coy were ordered to prolong the line to the MENIN RD and stragglers were ordered to be collected and organised to hold the line. It had now become clear that the offensive of the 7th Div had failed as the enemy were still holding a group of pillboxes south of, and abutting on the MENIN RD about J.21.d.80.75. An attempt was made by O.C. C Coy to seize these pillboxes but this attempt failed.

The next day, 27 October, the War Diary concludes:

> The Btn carried out this attack under extremely unfavourable conditions. The weather had been very bad for the preceding three weeks, and the mud in places was thigh deep. Rifles and Lewis guns became choked with mud owing to the men falling down during the advance. The 7th Div on the right flank did not capture and hold the group of pillboxes

> on the MENIN RD, about J.21.d.80.75., and consequently the assaulting Coys of the Btn were enfiladed by M.G. and rifle fire from there. 335 O/R's became casualties ...

One of those casualties was Private Arthur Cull, then aged 32. He was reported missing and for several weeks his wife waited in great anxiety hoping he was a prisoner. He was presumed killed in action but his body was not recovered. He is commemorated on the Tyne Cot Memorial, Zonnebeke, Belgium, panel 106 to 108.

Walter Cutting – A Casualty of the Third Battle of Ypres

On the same day that Arthur Cull was posted missing believed killed in action, another man with Stoke Poges connections, serving in another regiment, was also killed in the same battle.

He was Walter Fred Cutting, a private in the South Staffordshire Regiment. Nothing is known of Walter's Stoke Poges connection. He was a Suffolk man born in West Stow in that county, the son of Walter and Eleanor Cutting, themselves Suffolk folk.

Walter was living in Stoke Poges when he enlisted but we do not know the nature of his employment. Why he left Suffolk and moved to Stoke Poges is also a mystery but he was only 18 years of age when he was killed in the Third Battle of Ypres.

He was not shown on any of the monthly lists published in the Parish Magazine of men serving in the war. Neither was his name on the draft list of the Roll of Honour of names of those from Stoke Poges who died. This list was published in the Stoke Poges parish magazine of April 1919 and local people were invited to rectify any omissions. A revised list, published the next month, included the name of Cutting but his initials are shown incorrectly as V.F. instead of W.F. on the Memorial Tablet in St Giles' Church.

The War Diary of the 1st Battalion of the South Staffordshire Regiment sets out a narrative of operations for 26 October 1917, written by the Commanding Officer, Lieut. Colonel A.B. Beauman:

> 1. The forming up went off without incident, in spite of a very bright moon. There was a little shelling about 3.0 a.m. but only a few casualties were caused.
>
> 2. At zero the advance began. Heavy machine gun fire immediately opened on our lines, and a medium barrage came down along the whole front ridge, being somewhat severe about Bn. H.Q.
>
> 3. C Coy. on the left made progress in spite of heavy casualties from machine gun fire until within about 50 yards BERRY COTTS. Here very strong opposition was met with – stick bombs were freely used by the enemy and the attack was swept by machine gun fire from BERRY COTTS and LEWIS HOUSE. The mud had by now rendered most of the rifles and Lewis guns useless, and the Coy. strength was about one officer and 20 other ranks. No further progress could be made and the remains of the Coy. lay in shell holes until an opportunity could be found by retiring to the original front line.

4. D Coy. in the centre met with very strong opposition from HAMP FM. and suffered heavy casualties from cross machine gun fire. They could make no progress after advancing about 50 yards in front of our original front line.

5. B Coy. on the left suffered less from machine gun fire than the other Coys, being protected to a certain extent by lie of the ground. In consequence, they were able to make a determined attack on their objective THE MOUND which is a more important feature in the ground than would be imagined from the map. THE MOUND was strongly held by the enemy, and heavy fighting ensued. After a prolonged and desperate struggle, during which both officers and all the senior NCO's were killed or wounded, B Coy. now under the command of a Corporal carried their objective.

The enemy retired, leaving many dead and a heavy machine gun behind them. The position was consolidated, and messages sent back for reinforcements. Unfortunately, all the runners sent back became casualties, and no message reached Bn. H.Q. During the afternoon our artillery persistently shelled this position, and owing to their isolation the remnants of B Coy. were compelled to fall back at dusk.

The captured machine gun was destroyed before the position was evacuated.

6. By dusk, what was left of the Battalion was back on the original front line and was reorganised as far as possible.

The battalion was relieved at 11 p.m. by a battalion of the Manchester Regiment.

The next day, Major-General T.R.Shoubridge, CMG, DSO, Commanding 7th Division wrote to Lieut. Colonel Beauman as follows:

Dear Beauman,

I have just seen the Army Commander. Though he regrets we did not get our objective as much as we do ourselves, he fully realises that officers and men did all that was humanly possible in the face of great difficulties.

He also told me that the enemy had a railway reserve between MENIN and PASSCHENDAELE intending to employ it at the most threatened point. Our attack showed such determination that he retained all reserves opposite us. This helped the Canadians materially to gain and hold their objectives. Therefore we did not fight in vain.

The 7th Division has taken hard knocks before but it never loses its splendid spirit, and yesterday's battle will only be an incentive to get our own back on the next opportunity.

Will you convey the contents of this letter to all officers, N.C.O's and men, and also tell them how proud I am of the way in which they went forward under the worst conditions of mud and fire and would not give in until they died or stuck in the mud. No soldiers can do more.

Yours sincerely
(sd) Herbert Shoubridge.

Walter Cutting, of course, did not hear the contents of the letter read out; he was one of the fatal casualties and his body was not recovered. He is commemorated on the Tyne Cot Memorial, Zonnebeke, Belgium, panel 90 to 92 and 162 to 162A.

Henry Dancer – The Assault on the Petit Couronne

Henry James Dancer was born in 1890 in Stoke Poges, but his parents, David and Mary Dancer, were living in Fulmer at the time of the 1901 census.

Henry became a gardener and met Jane Friend who was also in domestic service. The couple worked at various houses around the country, married in 1912, and moved to Bells Hill. They had two daughters, Maisie born 1913 and Doris Mary born 1915. In December 1915 their father joined the Oxford and Bucks Light Infantry.

85 *Henry Dancer.*

Henry wrote home from Salonika at Christmas 1916 that he was having a rough time in the trenches, being up to his waist in mud and water, serving with the 7th Battalion of the Oxford and Bucks Light Infantry. 'But', he added, 'we must hang on for King and Country.' According to the Regimental Chronicle in November 1916 he was in the Doldzeli trenches with enemy artillery active day and night. He was back in the trenches from 10 to 16 December.

He and his comrades were out of the trenches for Christmas. The Regimental Chronicle recorded the event: – 'December 25th – cold but fine. After Church Parade C and D Companies played an exciting game of football, which ended in a draw. Everyone had an excellent Christmas dinner, including a liberal allowance of plum pudding provided by the *Daily Telegraph* and *Daily News* and the day was brought to a close with a most successful camp-fire concert.'

Private Henry Dancer lost his life on 9 May 1917 in an assault on a hill known as Petit Couronne, near Lake Doiran in northern Greece. Two other Stoke Poges men, Henry Fleet and Frederick King, also in the 7th Battalion of the Oxford and Bucks Light Infantry, lost their lives in the same action. His sergeant wrote to Jane Dancer:

> It will be some slight consolation to you in your great loss to know he passed away without any suffering. He was buried in an English cemetery by the side of his comrades. He was very popular with both officers and men in his Company, and he will be greatly missed by all the fellows in his platoon who send their deepest sympathy to you in your great bereavement.

Given the account of the battle, the reality was great suffering with heavy casualties and a number of his fellow soldiers being killed.

Henry is incorrectly described on the St Giles' Church Memorial Tablet as being in the Royal Berkshire Regiment. However, he has the distinction of being remembered on two memorials: St Giles and St James' Church, Fulmer.

Henry Dancer is buried in the Doiran Military Cemetery, Greece, grave reference VI.J.33. It was formed at the end of 1916 as a cemetery for the Doiran front. Most of the graves resulted from the fighting of April and May 1917, the attacks on the Petit Couronne. Jane Dancer died in Camberwell, London, in 1958.

Thomas Denteith – Emigrated to Australia

It is a mystery as to why Thomas Denteith is recorded on the St Giles' Church Memorial Tablet. Thomas Denteith was born near Manchester in 1874 and served in the 3rd Hussars as a regular soldier for seven years, possibly from 1892 when he was 18.

The Parish Magazine in July 1919 reported, some two years after the event, Thomas Denteith's death in action on 11 April 1917, serving as a private in the 16th Battalion of the Australian Infantry. It recalled that he resided for a time in Stoke Poges and emigrated to Australia with the son of Mr John Ayres.

The Ayres family, market gardeners, had a smallholding at Woodbine Cottages, two semi-detached properties, the other being owned by another market gardener, John Billings. These cottages still exist though much enlarged.

The original owner was George Parker. He and his wife Sophia had four daughters. Three of them left home leaving Maria to look after her father when her mother died. John Ayres worked for Parker and married Maria around 1892. They took over the business when George died and they had two sons, George and William.

George Parker Ayres emigrated to Australia with Thomas Denteith in 1912 when Denteith was 38 and Ayres 18. It may be that the father was much happier with his son going with an older more experienced man who would look out for him. In the event, they appear to have gone separate ways when they reached Australia.

Both Thomas Denteith and George Ayres served in the Australian Army and Ayres saw active service on the Somme in France. After the war, George Parker Ayres became a successful Australian farmer, starting with 58 acres. Today the family has 1,600 acres. He rarely talked about the war but, in later years, mentioned that he had lost too many friends and was thankful to have survived. He became a respected figure and deputy president of the Albany Shire Council. He died in 1974, aged 80.

Thomas Denteith's occupation when he enlisted was mill hand. Since his address was given as Kauri Timber P.O., Barabup, Western Australia, he evidently worked at the Barabup Mill, owned by the Kauri Timber Company. This was one of a number of 'timber settlements', which appeared in the late 19th early 20th centuries, and eventually faded away, largely as a result of environmental campaigns to save the native forests.

Thomas Denteith enlisted 7 May 1916 when he was 41, evidently prompted by his previous military service and sense of patriotism. Yet in just under a year, having arrived in France 16 January 1917, he was killed in action on 11 April 1917 in the Battle of Arras. He left a widow Adelaide and a son. His grandson remembers his father mentioning that he collected his father's medals and Memorial Scroll for his mother.

It is probable that William Ayres, who continued his market garden in Stoke Poges until the 1940s, nominated Thomas Denteith for inclusion on the Memorial Tablet in St Giles. More poignantly, he is one of the 10,000 Australian soldiers commemorated on the Villers-Bretonneux Memorial, Somme, France.

George Didcock – An Influenza Victim

George William Didcock was a private in the 11th Battalion Royal Fusiliers. He was the son of F. Didcock of Wexham Street, Stoke Poges. He volunteered at the outbreak of war.

We know little about George. He was wounded towards the close of 1917 and he died 14 July 1918, aged 26, following an attack of influenza. He was unmarried and is buried in Pernois British Cemetery, Halloy-Les-Pernois, Somme, France, grave reference II.E.14.

James Evans – First Day of the Battle of the Somme

James Evans came from Bilston in Staffordshire and had been a regular soldier, having enlisted in 1900. Most of his service had been in Egypt, and he was on the reserve at the outbreak of war. He was a lance sergeant in the 2nd Battalion of the Royal Berkshire Regiment when he died.

86 *James Evans.*

He married Lilian Turner, known as Lily, a Stoke Poges girl. The family lived in Hockley Hole. Jim was well known in the army and civilian life as a keen footballer. At the time of the Somme battle he had only just been discharged from hospital after being wounded.

The battle of the Somme lasted from July until November 1916. It began on 1 July when a bombardment, lasting just over one hour, fired almost a quarter million of shells at the enemy, so ferocious that it was heard in London. Ten mines being exploded under the enemy trenches followed it. Ten minutes later, at 7.30 a.m., on that bright Saturday morning, and as the whistles were blown, the troops went over the top across an 18-mile front.

> As they went over the top, most British troops carried with them about sixty six pounds' weight of equipment; a rifle, ammunition, grenades, rations, a waterproof cape, four empty sandbags, a steel helmet, two gas helmets, a pair of goggles against tear gas, a field dressing, a pick or a shovel, a full water bottle and a mess tin.*

This weight made it difficult to walk at more than a slow pace and made them easy targets for the enemy rifle and machine-gun fire.

The War Diary of the 2nd Battalion of the Berkshires sets out this graphic account:

* Gilbert, Martin, *First World War* (1994).

> Attack on OVILLERS. The Battalion took up its assembly positions in accordance with Brigade Operation Order No.100 – The 2nd Bn. LINCOLNSHIRE REGT was on our left and the 2nd Bn. DEVONSHIRE REGT on right.
>
> Our own wire was not sufficiently cut and parties were immediately sent out by Companies to clear it. At 6.25 am the intensive bombardment began as scheduled. At about 7.15 am the enemy opened rifle and machine gun fire on our line; this fire was probably drawn by the 2nd DEVON REGT which at about this time attempted to line up in front of their parapet. At 7.20 am Companies began filing down trenches and getting ready for the assault. At 7.30 am the three assaulting Companies advanced to attack the GERMAN line. They were met by intense rifle and machine gun fire, which prevented any of the waves reaching the enemy lines. A little group on the left of the Battalion succeeded in getting in, but were eventually bombed out.

The distance they had to cross between the front lines was no more than 200 yards.

This is how a German soldier saw those next few minutes:

> ... A series of extended lines of infantry were seen moving forward from the British trenches. The front line appeared to continue without end to right and left. It was quickly followed by a second line, then a third and fourth. They came on at a steady easy pace as if expecting to find nothing alive in our front trenches. 'Get ready' was passed along our front. A few moments later, when the leading British line was within a hundred yards the rattle of machine-gun fire broke out along the whole line. Red rockets sped into the blue sky as a signal to our artillery, and immediately afterwards a mass of shells from the German batteries burst among the advancing lines. Whole sections seemed to fall. The advance rapidly crumpled under this hail of shells and bullets. All along the line men could be seen throwing up their arms and collapsing, never to move again.
>
> The 2nd Royal Berkshire Regiment had gone into action with a strength of 24 officers and 823 other ranks. By 9.00 am they had left only four officers and 386 other ranks. Of their 457 casualties, 161 officers and men were killed, including Sergeant Evans. No part of the German front line trench in this sector of the battle front was captured and held on 1st July.*

Sergeant Jim Evans' body was not recovered and his name is recorded on the Thiepval Memorial, Somme, France, pier and face 11 D. He was 32 years of age.

William George Evered – Discharged as Unfit

The Memorial Tablet in St Giles' Church records 'G.E. Evered, Spr., R.E'. It is possible that these are the wrong initials and should refer to W.G. Evered. As early as April 1915 the Parish Magazine recorded two men serving with the

* Harvey, Trevor, 'Battle of the Somme', *Stoke Poges Parish Newsletter*, No79, June 1986.

name of Evered, both sappers in the Royal Engineers and both probably known as George. After May 1916, however, only one Evered continued to be listed in the Parish Magazine and he was G.E. Evered.

George E.Evered, the son of Arthur Daniel Evered, was born 3 February 1897 and lived at 4 Harding Cottages, Wexham Street. He would have been only 21 in 1918 and it is likely he survived the war but there are no surviving service records for him.

William George Evered was also born in Wexham Street, Stoke Poges, in 1880, the son of Albert and Anne Evered. He enlisted on 20 February 1915 giving his grandfather Charles Stevens as his next of kin. He was then 37, 5ft 8in tall; weight 138 lbs with normal vision and good physical development. He was single and his trade was given as 'rough carpenter'.

William George became a sapper in the Royal Engineers but was discharged in November 1917 no longer being physically fit for war service. His service records state that he was suffering from myalgia, which originated in January 1917 and was not the result of ordinary military service but aggravated by it. It was, according to these records, impossible to state if it was permanent. William had been admitted to hospital several times with myalgia, malaria and rheumatism, including three months in Bath taking the waters.

William George Evered died 25 October 1918, aged 39, and was buried 29 October in St Giles' Churchyard and, although his grave has not been identified, the entry on the church card index, number 69, records the burial of William George Rolfe Evered. His death is also recorded in the official register of deaths, the only local Evered who died at this time. The Commonwealth War Graves Commission does not list him or the other Evered on their Debt of Honour Register.

Although in May 1918 the Parish Magazine recorded that Sapper G.E. Evered had been invalided for some months owing to injury sustained by a fall of stores and had served in Salonika, a few months later, in November 1918, it recorded 'As we go to press we learn of the death of Sapper G. Evered, of Wexham Street, who was invalided recently'. Since there is only one Evered recorded as having died, and even though, according to his records, Sapper William George did not serve in Salonika, nevertheless we believe that he is the Evered commemorated on the Memorial Tablet.

Henry George Fleet – The Assault on the Petit Couronne

Born in Stoke Poges in 1879, Henry Fleet was the son of Alfred and Harriet Fleet who, at the time of the 1901 census, were living in Hockley Hole, roughly where Hockley Lane is situated now. He left the local school aged 12 to work as an agricultural boy, but by 1901 Henry was a bricklayer. He married Edith Isabel Elderfield and worked for five years for Wilberforce Bryant at Stoke Park and for the last 15 years for Deverill, a Slough builder.

His brother Albert, also a bricklayer, served in the South Wales Borderers, was wounded in 1915 and invalided out of the army. Henry volunteered early in the war, served in the Royal Engineers and was then discharged for munitions work. In July 1916 he enlisted in the Oxford and Bucks Light Infantry and in October 1916 sailed for Salonika.

87 *Henry Fleet with his younger sisters, Laura born 1880 and Lena born 1885.*

The Parish Magazine in July 1917 reported him as missing since 9 May. It was hoped he was a prisoner and had not yet been permitted to write. However, in October the Parish Magazine reported: 'It is with deep regret that we learn that the War Office now place among the killed Private Fleet, who has been missing since 9th May 1917.' The Magazine recalled his letter thanking the parish for his Christmas parcel when he wrote: 'Everyone will be pleased when it is all over and we are home again.'

Mrs Fleet took the editor of the Parish Magazine to task the next month writing that they were mistaken in stating that the War Office had assumed that Private Fleet, who is missing, had been killed. The Magazine expressed its regret that their error had caused any distress. It was, of course, not an error; he had been killed in the assault of 9 May 1917 on the hill known as Petit Couronne, near Lake Doiran in northern Greece. Two other men from Stoke Poges, Henry Dancer and Frederick King, were killed in the same action.

Henry Fleet was 38 when he lost his life, leaving a widow and children living in Wexham Street. He is commemorated on the Doiran Memorial, Greece.

William Gale – Severely Wounded on the Somme

William Gale, like the rest of his family, was born in Stoke Poges. The family lived at 3, West End, Stoke Poges, opposite Gladstone Cottages and Winterclyde.

William, a reservist with previous military service, was recalled at the beginning of the war and joined the 1st Battalion of the Royal Berkshire Regiment. He went to France 12 September 1914 and was wounded in the arm. He recovered from his wound and was moved to the 2nd Battalion. By 1917 his two brothers Bert, born 1895, and Arthur, born 1898, had joined up. Bert served in the Bucks Battalion, and Arthur in the Royal Navy,

William was wounded in the battle for Pallas Trench on 5 March 1917. On 17 March 1917 his parents received the dreaded letter telling them of William's death. The Parish Magazine reported it:

> Everyone will feel the deepest sympathy with Mr. and Mrs Gale, of West End, at the loss of their son, Private W. Gale, Royal Berkshire Regiment who died of wounds received in action on March 12th. The Chaplain writes 'He was brought into the New Zealand Hospital late on Sunday night suffering from a very severe wound in the left knee; he was just alive, and that was all, when he arrived, and died just before

> midnight. I buried him in the military cemetery in Amiens, where his grave is marked with a cross with his name and regiment on it.' Amiens is a large town with nearly 80,000 inhabitants, and the graves of the English soldiers are sure to be well cared for ...

Private William Gale is buried in St Pierre Cemetery, Amiens, Somme, France, grave reference VIII.B.1. His two brothers survived the war.

Walter Gutteridge – A Correspondent from the Front

Walter Gutteridge was born in 1887 in Langley, the son of George and Fanny Gutteridge. His father was born in Farnham Royal and his mother in Stoke Poges. It was a large family and there were six sons who served in the war. The family lived on Bells Hill.

Walter joined the army in 1905, when he was 18, serving for three years in the 2nd Battalion of the Oxford and Bucks Light Infantry. After leaving the army in January 1908, he worked as a gardener for Colonel Legge at Fulmer Gardens until January 1909 when he joined the Bucks Constabulary. He was described in police records as being 5ft 10in. in height, oval visage, fresh complexion, grey eyes and brown hair.

He started as a constable 3rd class and it took him four years to become a constable 1st class. Just before the outbreak of war, his pay was 26 shillings per week. His service was in the Wycombe area. On 4 August 1914 he was called upon to rejoin the army – the day war was declared.

Walter returned to his old regiment, the Oxford and Bucks Light Infantry, and was posted to France on 14 August 1914. He sent very descriptive letters from the front, which were published in the Parish Magazine.

9 February 1915:

> We have just come out of the firing line and we are back in reserve now. I had a very near go once lately. A party of us was in an old farmhouse making some tea, when suddenly a shell came through the roof and exploded in the next room. Pieces of tile and bricks flew in all directions, but luckily none of us was hit. But, of course, we are quite used to this sort of thing as it is so frequent, and we stayed and enjoyed our tea and then went back to our trenches.

9 March 1915:

> I am pleased to say we are all enjoying good health – the boys of Stoke. We came out of the trenches last evening, and looked a pretty sight. We were covered from head to feet in clay. We have been to a different part of the line this time from where we were when I last wrote. The trenches were among the brickfields, and a rather warm quarter, and we had some exciting times during our stay in the trenches. I was very much interested in the paper one morning, when a shell burst on top of the trench and cut the dirt all over me, so I simply passed the remark, 'Thank You,' and went on reading. On another occasion a shell burst and blew 5 sandbags on to my chum on my right and almost buried him, but luckily none of us was hurt.

30 March 1915:

> We came out of the trenches on the night of the 28th, so we all met together last evening, Pte Elderfield saw Pte J R Groves and the 7th City of London Battalion, whilst he was in the trenches, as the 7th came into the trenches with us. He was quite well and wished to be remembered to his Stoke and Wexham friends.
>
> One night an officer and three of us went out in front of our lines with intention of getting to the German lines (which are about 250 yards away) to gather what information we could. It was a terrible wet night, so you can guess what we were like after crawling and lying about ground that had been cultivated last year. After about half-an-hour crawling about we suddenly heard a German working party on in front of their trench. Of course, when a working party is out, they have a covering party out in front of them in case they are attacked. We crawled along to within 30 yards of their covering party, when a night-light went up some distance off, and we could see them all lying down.
>
> Our officer had got some good information and we returned to our lines. The next night as soon as their working party started, our artillery gave them a few shells to go on with. Our officer had given the guns the exact spot, for we could see the shells bursting right over them; so you may guess there were a few casualties, and we didn't hear any more of the working party that night.

14 May 1915:

> We took part in this great battle, which started at daybreak on Sunday last (9th). Of course I can give no details, but our Division (2nd) was in support of the 1st Division, which made the attack. We relieved them from the firing line on Sunday night and held the trenches till relieved. At present we are in reserve. Our artillery must have killed thousands of Germans. The guns kept up a continual fire all day yesterday. I am pleased to say the casualties in our regiment are light. Kind regards to all.

The great battle to which Walter referred was the battle of Frezenberg, 8 to 13 May, one of the series of battles in April and May 1915, which was termed 'Second Ypres'.

22 May 1915:

> We have been in the thick of it lately and have done well. We gave the Germans a surprise last Saturday night. We rushed them and captured two lines of trenches and a machine gun. No doubt you have seen where the 1st. Army has been fighting: we seem to be driving the Germans back all along the line now.

1 June 1915:

> I am glad to say Pte. Elderfield is going on well; he is attached to my company. I have not heard any news from L.-Cpl. Davis, but Pte.

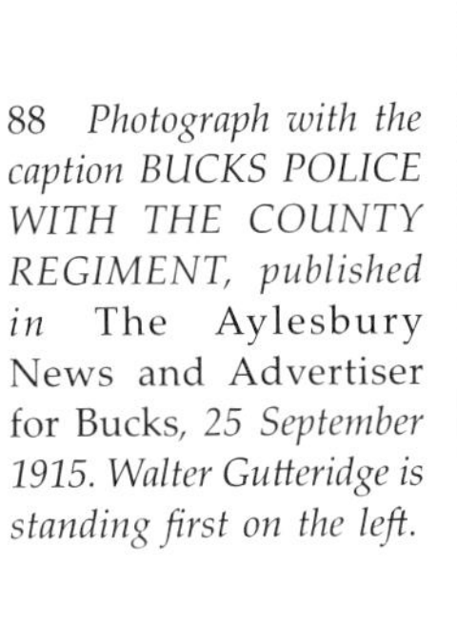

88 *Photograph with the caption BUCKS POLICE WITH THE COUNTY REGIMENT, published in* The Aylesbury News and Advertiser for Bucks, *25 September 1915. Walter Gutteridge is standing first on the left.*

Elderfield saw him when he was down at the base and he was going on all right then. We all sincerely hope Pte. Isbell is doing well. We are at a different part of the firing line, where we have never been before. We had a very trying march to get here, about 20 miles and a very hot day. We got here about midnight and went straight into the trenches. They are very good trenches and amongst the chalk – so you can guess we look a pretty good sight. We have been made up to strength so we are quite ready for another advance.

5 June 1915 and Pte. Thompson writes with news of Pte Gutteridge:

Pte. Gutteridge has been wounded in the foot, the last day we were in the trenches. We were relieving the French and it was on the fourth day that he got wounded with a piece of shell fired from what we call a 'whizz-bang' (or trench mortar). He got one piece of shell out himself and the doctor pulled out three pieces and then there was one piece left in – so you can tell it was a nasty wound; but not very serious. He walked from the firing line to the dressing room by himself.

6 June 1915 Pte. W. Gutteridge resumes his letter writing:

I have arrived in England and am pleased to say my wound is not very serious. I had a lovely journey over; arrived at Le Havre about 4 p.m. Friday (4th) had my wounds dressed and then went straight on board the S.S. Asturias and arrived at Southampton about 9 a.m. this morning (Sunday).

10 June 1915:

I have had an operation and had the pieces of shell extracted and I shall be able to get about again in about a week's or a fortnight's time.

> Before I close I should like to mention a little about the splendid work our 'Red Cross Society' are doing – both at the front and at home; with reference to the soldiers in the trenches and the wounded being conveyed to the base hospitals and hospitals at home.
>
> When I was in the trenches, one of the Society's motor-vans used to come up to within two miles of the firing line, and bring us loaves of bread, eggs, and cocoa and if it had not been for this we should have had to have biscuits for several days together. Then there are the Red Cross Nurses on the trains in France, attending to the wounded as they are conveyed to the base hospitals.
>
> I heard one poor fellow, who was in the same carriage as myself, say how nice it was to hear the gentle voice of an English lady.
>
> The Nurses are also in attendance on the hospital-ship coming over to England and on the trains which convey the wounded from the ship to the various hospitals in England and they make everything so comfortable; and when the trains stop at the stations there are all kinds of refreshments, etc. distributed all along the train by this Society.

In August Pte Gutteridge was passed fit for duty and posted to Cambridge Barracks, Portsmouth with the 3rd Battalion, Oxford and Bucks Light Infantry where Harold Skues and several other Stoke Poges men were in the same battalion. He was expecting to be in a draft being sent to the Persian Gulf.

The next news of Gutteridge was on 22 November from the Balkans where he was attached to the 6th Battalion of the Munster Fusiliers, who had fought so magnificently in rearguard actions in the Balkans. The next year, 1916, he was promoted lance corporal and subsequently corporal.

21 March 1916 from Salonika:

> I hope all Stoke and Wexham friends are well. I have not met any of the Stoke lads out here yet, but I hear the 7th Battalion are close to where we are now. It is quite a pretty sight round our camp, as we have all got flower beds round our tents, and the wild flowers here are far better than those in England, primroses especially.

In the autumn of 1916 Walter was promoted to sergeant but, sadly, his promotion was short-lived; he was killed on 3 October 1916. The Parish Magazine of December 1916 contained the following tribute:

> Mr and Mrs Gutteridge have the deepest sympathy of all their fellow-parishioners, and it is our prayer that the other five sons they have given to the Army, three of whom have been wounded, may long be spared to them.

Walter Gutteridge seems to have had the gift of drawing out the regard and affection of others, and this is borne out by the following testimony written by the officer commanding his company:

> His death is a great blow to me and the other officers of his company who had formed the highest opinion of him. The N.C.O's and men too had learnt to respect him as a very capable leader. It is impossible, I

> know, to offer any consolation, but I should like you to know that he died a hero's death, gallantly leading his Machine Gun Section. His comrades buried him near the place where he fell and put a little cross over his grave.

The January 1917 issue of the Magazine had this tribute from the Superintendent of the County Police Station at High Wycombe who wrote to Mrs Gutteridge:

> May I ask you to accept the sincere sympathy of all here in your sad bereavement. I am very sorry to know that we shall not have him back with us. He was a capable police officer, and always carried out his duties in a most satisfactory manner. The whole of the Division have missed his cheerful countenance from the time he first left us.

Walter, who was unmarried, was killed, aged 29, in Greek Macedonia, and in a battle to capture a village called Yenikeui on the road to Seres in Northern Greece. He is buried in Struma Military Cemetery, Greece; grave reference III. J.14. This section of the cemetery consists entirely of graves brought in from the battlefields and front-line cemeteries. The other five sons of Fanny Gutteridge, one of whom was awarded the Military Medal, all returned home safely. She herself died, age 68, one year after the war ended.

Harry Hammond – The Attack on Bellewaarde Farm

Harry Hammond's connection with Stoke Poges was his employment as a gardener at Stoke Place, the Howard-Vyse estate.

Harry was born in 1891 in Knutsford, Cheshire. His father Joseph, a gas stoker, was also a Knutsford-born man, his mother Martha coming from Wrexham. At the time of the 1901 census the family consisted of Harry, then aged 10, James eight, William seven and Joseph five, all born in Knutsford. Sometime after 1901 Martha Hammond died and his father remarried. His next of kin in the Commonwealth War Graves Commission records was given as Mrs Francis Hammond of 6 Old Market Place, Knutsford, his stepmother.

In September 1914, Harry enlisted in the Oxford and Bucks Light Infantry and served in France with the 5th Battalion as a lance-corporal. He was wounded in the attack on Bellewaarde Farm in the Ypres Sector on 25 September 1915.

This was a diversionary attack in support of the main action, the Battle of Loos. It was made by 42nd Infantry Brigade, 14th Division, with the 5th Battalion of the Oxford and Bucks being the centre battalion in the attack. The failure of the brigade to hold the line after it had been captured was due to one company and a platoon of another company being almost wiped out by enemy artillery while lying out in the open prior to the assault. The result was that only two corporals were left to lead the attack with about 20 men. These survivors were a good deal unnerved by the explosion of a mine close to them under the enemy redoubt, and they went too far to the left and joined with the 9th Rifle Brigade. Although the right column succeeded in reaching the enemy second line, they were forced back by a very strong counter-attack. Prisoners revealed that the enemy had been expecting the attack for three days and this explained the strength and rapidity of their counter-attack with fresh troops.

The gap in the centre, however, was fatal. The enemy realised this weakness and reacted to it. In the assault 13 officers out of 15, and 463 other ranks out of 769, were killed or wounded.

Harry was one of the wounded and he was sent to a hospital in London where an operation was performed and an expanding bullet was taken from his wound. Unfortunately, haemorrhage set in and he died cheerful and plucky to the last. Just three days before his death he wrote very cheerily to a friend, saying he was back in England for a short stay, having managed to get a bit of shrapnel in his left side. 'But' he added, 'we showed them the way to go.'

Harry Hammond died 3 October 1915, aged 24, and four days later was buried with full military honours in Tottenham and Wood Green Cemetery, Middlesex, grave reference gen. 7333 (Screen Wall). The *Slough Observer* recorded that Mr Page, head gardener at Stoke Place, attended the funeral representing the Howard-Vyse family and Harry's fellow gardeners. He laid a wreath of flowers that Harry had helped to grow on his grave.

Claude Hanbury – 2nd Battalion, Irish Guards

Claude Everard Robert Hanbury was born on 8 August 1893 in Ascot, the eldest son of Ashley and Amy Hanbury. The family moved to Stoke Green. He was educated at Cheam and Haileybury. His father, a paper merchant, died in January 1914. Claude was in South Africa when war broke out but returned immediately and was commissioned in the Royal Field Artillery.

In July 1915 Hanbury, who was 6ft 3in tall, transferred to the 1st Battalion of the Irish Guards. He completed a bomb instructor's course and then served from October 1915 until March 1916 with the British Expeditionary Force. On 3 March 1916 he was injured in his hand and leg when, during a practice he was conducting with live bombs, one prematurely exploded. This accident so severely injured one officer that he died within an hour and two others, including the padre, were also injured. Hanbury returned home to hospital in Highgate. This delayed his return to active service until early December 1916 when he joined the 2nd Battalion in France.

89 *Captain Claude Hanbury.*

The 2nd Battalion had been formed, following the King's approval, on 18 July 1915. Lord Kitchener who believed that the high standards of the Guards would have a beneficial effect on other formations of the New Army, Kitchener's volunteers, inspired this move. John Kipling, the son of Rudyard Kipling, and killed in action at the age of 18 in September 1915, was one of its officers.

90 *The family of Ashley and Amy Hanbury in 1911. Left to right, Madeline, Joan, Claude, Ashley with the family's youngest child name not known, Amy and Vera.*

The month after he returned to France, in January 1917, Claude was slightly wounded when a shell hit a carrying-party close to him.

Later that year, on 9 October 1917, Claude Hanbury, then a captain, was killed in action on the Ypres Salient. He was 24 years of age. The attack in which he was killed was an action to cross the Broembeek, a river whose banks were mostly marshy, to advance a little more than three thousand yards to the edge of the Forest of Houthulst.

The 2nd Battalion War Diary entry for that day reads:

> The morning broke fine and clear and the ground was drying well under a good wind. Zero hour was fixed for 5.20 a.m. at which hour it was sufficiently light to see about 200 – 300 yds. The opening of the intense 18-pdr barrage was the signal for the infantry to leave their trenches and advance to the attack.
>
> The BROEMBEEK was crossed without any difficulty. We were now in touch with the 1st Bt. Scots Guards on our right and the French on our left. The attack proceeded without a hitch, all pill boxes being rushed and captured without much difficulty.
>
> The first objective was gained on scheduled time, with few casualties. There was a pause and after 15 mins. no 1 and 2 coys. passed through no 3 and 4 coys. who were consolidating, and laying down under the barrage waited for it to roll back. When it lifted these 2 coys. advancing close to it, assaulted and captured the 2nd objective, arriving there on scheduled time.

C.E.R. Hanbury is buried in Canada Farm Cemetery, Elverdinghe, Ieper, Belgium, grave reference III.D.15. He is also commemorated on his parents' gravestone in St Giles' Churchyard.

Henry Holdship – Returned from the War Broken in Health

Henry Holdship is not recorded on the Commonwealth War Graves Commission Debt of Honour Register but when he died on 2 February 1920 the following month's issue of the Parish Magazine contained this entry:

The Roll of Honour:

> To our Roll must be added the names of the following soldiers, all from Farnham Road, who came back broken in health from the war, died in consequence of it.
>
> We commend them to the love and mercy of our God
>
> Archibald Mck Tyson
> Henry Holdship
> Alfred Gladstone Albrow

The three men had died within a few weeks of each other, after the Memorial Tablet (the Roll of Honour) had been erected in St Giles' Church.

Henry Holdship was 39 when he died. An old soldier, having first joined the Oxfordshire Light Infantry* at the age of 17 in 1897, he had served in India at well known stations such as Poona and Lucknow. He was described as being of fresh complexion, 5ft 6¾in in height, with brown hair, hazel eyes, weighing 133 lbs, and by trade a blacksmith. At the end of 1905 when he left the army he became a postman.

In December 1915 Henry re-enlisted in the Leicestershire Regiment as a private but he does seem to have been dogged by ill health. At the end of 1916 he was posted to France and served in the trenches. Six months later he was sent home suffering from trench foot. As a result of the wet, cold and insanitary conditions in the trenches many soldiers suffered this painful incapacity. It was particularly exacerbated when men were standing in waterlogged trenches for hours at a time. At first there was a loss of feeling in the feet; they would swell and go 'dead' and then burn like red-hot pokers. In extreme cases feet and legs were amputated.

Eventually it was realised that dry socks and rubbing whale grease in the feet two or three times a day was an essential preventive measure. A battalion at the front used ten gallons of whale oil a day for this process.

By the time of his demobilisation in March 1919, Henry was suffering from a number of ailments, including from June 1919 epileptic convulsions. A medical board assessed his disability at 20 per cent but that his medical condition was not the direct result of war service. Nevertheless, he still suffered from the effects of trench foot and needed to rest after walking. This medical board was held on 12 December 1919 and Henry died just two months later on 2 February 1920 of pneumonia.

Henry Holdship is buried in St Giles' Churchyard. Surely, Canon Barnett, the then Vicar of Stoke Poges, who himself spent long periods in France during the

---

* Henry Holdship enlisted in 1897 in the Oxfordshire Light Infantry, which was formed in 1881 as the county regiment of Oxfordshire and Buckinghamshire. It united two battalions, the 1st Battalion, a re-designation of the 43rd (Monmouthshire Light Infantry) Regiment of Foot and the 2nd Battalion, a re-designation of the 52nd (Oxfordshire Light Infantry) Regiment of Foot. In 1908 it became the Oxfordshire and Buckinghamshire Light Infantry.

war, knew these men and had observed their broken health. He was, therefore, able to make the judgement that led him to write as he did in the Parish Magazine that they should be added to the Roll of Honour.

Ernest Humphries – Gloucestershire Regiment

Ernest Humphries was born in Langley and his family lived on Bells Hill. He volunteered at the outbreak of the war and served for most of it in the front line.

As 1917 ended the Allies were expecting a major German offensive. The Allies were suffering a severe manpower shortage. Field Marshal Sir Douglas Haig, Commander-in-Chief of the British Expeditionary Force, had received a little over half of the reinforcements he had requested. In February and March 1918 among the measures to cope with these problems was the amalgamation of 38 battalions to form 19 battalions. Ernest Humphries' battalion, the 10th, became part of the 13th Gloucesters on 14 February 1918.

The Germans launched their Spring Offensive on 21 March 1918 and Ernest Humphries was posted missing on 4 April. For some weeks afterwards the family had hoped that he had been taken prisoner but these hopes were dashed when it was confirmed that he had been killed.

As a lad Ernest had worked for the Rev. J.F. Hoyle when he was the vicar of Stoke Poges, then for Dr Morriston-Davies and prior to enlisting was employed at Derry Mohr. He died 4 April 1918, aged 22. He was unmarried and is buried in Villers-Bretonneux Military Cemetery, Somme, France, grave reference IV.E.10. The German advance had ended on 23 April 1918 with the capture of the village of Villers-Bretonneux and its recapture the next day by the 4th and 5th Australian Divisions and units of the 8th and 18th Divisions.

Arthur James – The Oldest Volunteer from the Parish

Sapper Arthur James was born in 1870 and he was the oldest Stoke Poges man in the war. The son of Charles and Kate James of Wexham Street, at the time of the 1881 census he had two brothers, Charles born 1871, George born 1875 and a sister Emma born 1877. The family lived in Slough before moving to 4 Rose Cottage, Wexham Street.

Arthur, a labourer, joined a Labour Battalion of the Royal Engineers in September 1915 and was described as being 5ft 8in in height, girth 36in, complexion ruddy, grey eyes and dark brown hair.

He served in France for only ten months before being returned home and discharged as unfit on 16 November 1916. His illness originated in May 1916 in France but was not caused or aggravated by military service.

Arthur was diagnosed as suffering from cancer and, consequently, he was not eligible for a full pension. An appeal was made via Sir Matthew Nathan, Secretary to the Ministry of Pensions, to the Advisory Board. There is a note on Arthur's file that he was in St Bartholomew's Hospital, suffering agonies of pain, that nothing could be done for him, that his capacity for earning a livelihood was lessened by total incapacity and that he was a suitable case for consideration under regulations that permitted some discretion. The Board met in May 1917 and did make a favourable decision but Arthur died a month later on 5 June 1917.

The Parish Magazine contained this obituary:

> It is with deep regret that we record the death on June 5th, in a Home in Hampstead of Private Arthur James, of Wexham Street. He may certainly be said to have laid down his life for his King and Country. At the age of upwards of 46, when most men would have excused themselves, he volunteered in August 1915, and was for some time at the front until invalided six months ago with an incurable disease. Brought up in Slough he came to Stoke some five years ago and was employed by Messrs. Hartley of Wexham until he enlisted. His mortal remains were laid to rest in our Stoke Poges Graveyard on June 9th, the first of our soldiers who have fought in this war to find a resting place there.

Arthur James was 47 and the location of his grave is not shown on the churchyard plan. The Commonwealth War Graves Commission does not record his death.

Charles Jones Johnson – A South African

Charles Jones Johnson was a South African who served as a private in the 1st South African Infantry, 4th Regiment, which he joined in Durban in May 1917 when he was aged 25 years. He left Cape Town on 25 June 1917 on HMT *Ulysses*. He married Edith Mabel Werrell of Stoke Green Farm in St Giles' Church 26 October 1917, just a year before he was killed.

Charles Johnson was killed in action, 17 October 1918, in a battle to cross the River Selle and capture Le Cateau in northern France. At 8.45 a.m. on the morning of 17 October, having crossed to the east bank of the River Selle the previous evening, the South Africans advanced through thick mist across belts of single and double wire and heavy machine-gun fire from both flanks. They encountered a sunken road protected by a palisade where the 4th Regiment was held up and suffered many losses. Near the railway was a 60-yard deep belt of wire entanglements. Despite these obstacles the South Africans found a way through that had been made for German patrols and they reached the railway. It was during this fighting that Charles Johnson lost his life.

He was buried in Chateau Seydoux British Cemetery, Le Cateau, one of 41 South African soldiers, and, subsequently, reburied in Ors British Cemetery, Nord, France. His grave reference is A.14. Ors British Cemetery is also the resting place of Lieut Wilfred Owen, MC, killed in action on 4 November 1918. Shortly before his death Owen had written: 'Of this I am certain you could not be visited by a band of friends half as fine as surround me here.'

Edith Johnson's sister Winifred who married Robert Cowell was also widowed on 23 July 1918 (*see* pp. 87-8).

Arthur Grey King – Part of our Imperial Heritage

Arthur Grey King was born on 15 November 1871 in Windsor and, when he joined the Royal Marines in January 1890, he listed his occupation as a draper's porter. He is described as being 5ft 10in in height, of fresh complexion with dark brown hair and hazel eyes.

In the closing years of the 19th century Arthur had an adventurous life. The Royal Navy was an important instrument in wielding imperial power. In 1894 he was attached to HMS *St George*, the flagship on the South Africa station. The next year he took part in the Brass River punitive expedition.

King Koko, the chief of the Brass River people in Nigeria, had attacked a British trading post in West Africa and his appeal for more time to consider Admiral Bedford's demand for restitution was rejected. Arthur earned a Brass River clasp to his East and West Africa Medal (1887-1900)* for taking part in the punitive expedition.

In August of the same year he took part in the Mwele expedition. A British force was sent to capture Mwele, the stronghold of the Swahili rebel Mbarak. This force consisted of five cruisers, including Arthur King's ship HMS *St George*, 400 sailors and marines from the ships, 60 Sudanese askaris, 50 local askaris, 800 porters and a field gun, rocket tube and two Maxim guns.

The next year, 1896, he took part in what the Guinness Book of Records lists as the shortest war in history. This occurred when the Sultan of Zanzibar, Hamad, died on 25 August and the British declared his cousin Hamoud as successor. Another cousin, Khaled, considered he had a better claim and with 2,000 supporters took over the palace, barring entrance to Sir Basil Cave, the acting British Consul. Since Zanzibar was a British protectorate this action was unacceptable. Cave called on the assistance of marines from three British ships in the harbour. At dawn Rear Admiral Rawson turned his guns on the palace and issued an ultimatum, either Khaled surrendered or the fleet would open fire. At 8 a.m. Khaled asked for talks but this request was curtly refused. At 9.02 a.m. the ships opened fire on the palace and at 9.40 a.m. Khaled surrendered, with the palace in ruins and 500 bodies in the debris.

In 1897 Arthur earned a second clasp to his East and West Africa Medal for taking part in the Benin expedition. This was another display of imperial power. The dispute related to trading interests. Britain had established a palm oil industry, palm oil being used in the manufacture of soap, but King Oba Ovonramwen of Benin sought to impose a customs levy. An impetuous officer, Lieut Phillips, advanced on Benin with a small force of ten British officers, 200 porters and a drum and fife band on what he claimed was a peace mission but what Oba viewed as an attack. Phillips and eight officers were killed. In February 1897 a force of 1,200 British troops and Africans ransacked Benin City, burned the King's palace and removed treasures and auctioned off most of them to pay for the cost of the punitive expedition.

Returning home Arthur married Elsie Grey Benham in October 1900, and the following year re-enlisted for another 10 years, becoming a reservist in 1911. He and Elsie Grey King lived for a time in Ragstone Road, Slough, where he was a member of the Slough Town Band, and then in Southall. His parents lived in Wexham Street, Stoke Poges.

Arthur was called back to service on the outbreak of the war and was with the Marine Division at the siege of Antwerp where he had several narrow escapes from death. By now a sergeant, he was aboard HMS *Bayano* when a German submarine, the *U27*, torpedoed her on 11 March 1915.

---

* The Stoke Poges Parish Magazine of April 1915, in its obituary, recorded that Arthur Grey King held the Ashanti Medal but as his service records confirm he held the East & West Africa Medal. In the book *British Battles & Medals* by Major L.L.Gordon, 1979, the author states: 'This medal is slightly thinner than that awarded for the Ashanti Campaign of 1873-74. In all other respects, including the ribbon, it is the same.'

The *Bayano* was a liner taken over early in the war to serve as an armed cruiser. She was on her way to Liverpool to coal when she was intercepted ten miles N.W. by W. of Corsewall Point, Galloway, and sunk. Attacked at 5.15 a.m. the *Bayano* sank very rapidly with only four officers and 22 ratings being saved. Fourteen officers and 181 ratings were lost. The SS *Castlereagh* arrived at the scene shortly after the sinking but the presence of the *U27* prevented her making a search.

As well as his campaign medals, Arthur Grey King, who was 42 when he died, had four good conduct badges. His wife had the distinction of a special message of condolence from the King and Queen. Sergeant King was buried in Southall Cemetery, Middlesex, grave reference C.62, his body having been recovered from the sea a week after the disaster. The Southall Town Band, of which he was a member, played the Dead March from 'Saul' at the funeral.

An interesting sequel to the sinking of the *Bayano* was that the *U27* was herself sunk some five months later in the Western Approaches by the Q ship HM Auxiliary Cruiser *Baralong*. The circumstances of the sinking caused the Germans to accuse the *Baralong*'s crew of murdering German sailors and breaching International Law.

Frederick King – The Assault on the Petit Couronne

Frederick John King was born in 1884 in Newton Longville in Buckinghamshire. The son of Thomas and Mary King of Bletchley, his father worked at Bletchley Park, his occupation being described in the 1901 census as a 'stationary engine driver'. Frederick's occupation then, when he was aged 17, was 'assistant gardener domestic'. According to the census he had a younger brother Arthur, then aged 13, and a sister, Emma aged 11.

91 *Newton Longville, where Frederick King was born.*

Frederick, who was unmarried, was foreman in the gardens at Stoke Place, the Howard-Vyse estate. Little else is known about him. Having been a foreman in civilian life, his promotion to sergeant indicates he was able and experienced in handling men.

Frederick King was killed 9 May 1917 in the same action as Henry Dancer and Henry Fleet. He is commemorated on the Doiran Memorial in Greece. This memorial stands near the Doiran Military Cemetery. The memorial is in the form of an obelisk, 12 metres high. Frederick King is also commemorated on the Bletchley St Mary War Memorial, which is situated on a triangular area off Church Green Road, Bletchley, at the entrance to St Mary's Church.

Alfred Joseph Lawrence – A Sailor who Fought on Land

Alfred Joseph Lawrence was aged only 20 when he died of wounds on 28 September 1918. Born in the village and educated in the Stoke Poges School, his family lived in West End, Rogers Lane. Before joining the Royal Navy 11 October 1916, Alfred had worked at Tithe Farm, Stoke Court and Stoke Park.

He was 5ft 3in in height, chest 32 inches, weight 106 lbs, fair complexion, dark brown hair and eyes but he was a non-swimmer. Alfred served in the Anson Battalion of the 63rd (Royal Naval) Division. Winston Churchill formed the 63rd (Royal Naval) Division as an infantry formation in 1914 continuing a tradition of employing ad-hoc groupings of sailors and marines in land operations. Mobilisation of naval reservists meant a surplus of men without space for them on the navy's ships. The battalions that were formed included the 8th later named the Anson Battalion. A few months before Lawrence joined, control of the Royal Naval Division was transferred to the War Office.

92 *Stoke Court, where Alfred Lawrence worked, was owned by the Allhusen family.*

93 *The* Dog and Pot. *Alfred Lawrence lived nearby.*

Alfred Lawrence took part in the battle at Passchendaele in October/November 1917 when he was badly gassed and sent home. He only returned to the front in August 1918 and was dangerously wounded on 27 September in the attack on the Hindenburg Line and died the next day at a casualty clearing station.

The Chaplain wrote to Mrs Lawrence:

> Suffering from severe wounds, he was practically unconscious when he arrived (at the Clearing Station) and was not suffering. He passed away quite peacefully a few hours later, early in the morning of September 28th. We buried him on September 28th in the British Military Cemetery near the Hospital. A little cross has been erected over his grave, which is clearly marked and will be kept tidy by the cemetery authorities.'

Able Seaman Alfred Lawrence is buried in Sunken Road Cemetery, Boisleux-St Marc, Pas-de-Calais and his grave reference is II.E.13. His elder brother William, a sergeant in the Hampshire Regiment, survived the war.

George Leslie – Killed on Sentry Duty in the Somme Sector

George Edward Leslie was born in Stoke Poges in 1882, the son of William and Louisa Leslie of Bells Hill. George had been the Colnbrook local postman for some 16 years, having transferred from Stoke Poges. He was not shown on the regular list that was published each month in the Parish Magazine of Stoke Poges men serving in the forces. However, probably due to his parents, he was recorded on the War Memorial Tablet.

After the Battle of the Somme, which lasted from 1 July until the middle of November 1916, there followed another difficult winter in the trenches. The struggle of the Somme battlefield had reduced the enemy's strength. From January until April 1917 the Allies gradually extended their front line. This was helped by the German decision to retire to a new and shorter defensive line they had prepared, known as the Siegfried Line to the Germans, and the Hindenburg Line to the British.

Nevertheless, during this period trench warfare continued and there were raids and counter-raids on trench positions. George Leslie's battalion, the 2/1st

Bucks Battalion of the Oxford and Bucks Light Infantry, was in Spuds sub section. After a heavy enemy artillery bombardment on 28 February 1917, lasting three hours, while he was on sentry duty with a Lewis gun team, an enemy shell buried him. 'With all possible speed he was dug out, but it was found the worst had happened.' The enemy raided the 2/4th Battalion of the Regiment located on the left but this was repulsed.

His Company Officer wrote: '... in him we have lost one of our very best men. He was always willing to do anything. He did his duty nobly.' His sergeant also wrote: '... as a soldier he was one of the keenest and always did his duty well. His loss in the Company is felt by all, and I am sure no man could have had more friends.'

Private George Leslie was buried just inside the trenches, and left a widow and two children. She was informed that the chaplain had consecrated his grave, which was duly registered but presumably lost subsequently hence his inclusion on the Thiepval Memorial, Somme, pier and face 10A and 10D.

Frederick Margetts – Died of Shrapnel Wounds

Frederick Margetts was born in Stoke Poges. His parents came from Oxfordshire and his father was a carpenter. The family lived in The Firs, Stoke Common. Freddy had a younger brother George and they were educated at Stoke Poges School.

Freddy was a leading boy in Sunday school under Mrs Blake, the then vicar's wife, and he also acted as a teacher. He worked at Stoke Court as a gardener when he left school and then at Hall Barn, Beaconsfield until he joined the army.

Freddy joined the 7th Battalion of the Rifle Brigade soon after the outbreak of war. He became a corporal and was wounded with five others by bursting shrapnel on the banks of the Yser Canal when returning from some trenches near the ruined village of La Brique. He was taken to the Red Cross Hospital at Etaples, near Boulogne, where he died, aged 27, on 13 December 1915.

94 *Fircroft House built in 1906 when it was known as 'The Firs'. The owner Mrs J.M. McNeile, who is seen with a friend standing in the grounds, took this photograph in 1908. Freddie Margetts' mother, who was a widow, was probably in service with Mrs McNeile. Fircroft is now divided into flats.*

95 This photograph of Fircroft House, dated Christmas 1911, shows that additions have been made to the house.

His mother received the customary letter of condolence from his platoon commander who wrote:

> Corporal Margetts was one of the best men in my platoon, and as a non commissioned officer, was of the greatest value to us both in and out of the trenches. When we were last up, especially, his indefatigable work was highly appreciated. He will be missed and mourned by officers and men alike.

Frederick Margetts is buried in Etaples Military Cemetery, Pas de Calais, France, grave reference VI.A.16.

William Mayne – A Casualty of the Battle of the Aisne

William Mayne was born in Ruscombe near Twyford, Berkshire, in 1884. We know from the census that in 1901 his family was living in Pit House on the Mapledurham Estate in Oxfordshire. His parents were Berkshire folk. William was then 16 and his occupation was listed as cattleman worker. There were four sisters – Ada 14, Alice 11, Mary two and Dora four months – and two brothers – Frederick nine and Lesley four.

At the outbreak of the First World War William, now 30 and married, was employed at Stoke Park. By this time the golf course had been established and William may well have been employed on the course.

He was a reservist, having joined the Oxford and Bucks Light Infantry on 6 November 1903, and was one of the first to respond to the general mobilisation. He joined the 2nd Battalion of the Oxford and Bucks Light Infantry.

General mobilisation had commenced on 5 August 1914, the day after war was declared. On 12 August the Battalion, as part of the 5th Infantry Brigade, 2nd Division, 1st Army Corps, left Cowley Barracks by train for embarkation to France. The King and Queen inspected the Regiment informally on parade to say goodbye.

The British Expeditionary Force arrived in France on the twelfth day after Germany declared war on France. The Germans were overrunning Belgium. The French advanced into Belgium to stop them. The task of the B.E.F. was

96 *Pontoons ready for the Front. The 2nd Battalion Diary of the Oxford and Bucks Light Infantry refers to the construction of a pontoon bridge to enable it to cross the Aisne.*

to prolong the French line to the north-west to prevent a wide enveloping movement on the Allies' left flank.

On 23 August the Battle of Mons began followed by the Allied retreat to the French frontier. By 30 August the German Army had driven the Anglo-French forces southwards across the River Aisne and the B.E.F. reached the north bank of the River Marne on 2 September. They crossed the river the next day blowing the bridges behind them.

For the 2nd Battalion of the Oxford and Bucks Light Infantry, the retreat from Mons ended on 5 September when they reached Chamblet. Between 25 August and 5 September they had retreated 178 miles in 12 marches and had one halt day. As Lieut-Colonel Davies noted in his diary: 'Not a very long distance, but very long hours under arms; hardly any sleep, and broiling hot weather. Never in my life have I felt anything like the degree of tiredness that I felt in this retreat.'

There were several Stoke Poges men serving with the 2nd Battalion including Private Ted Elderfield and the two Gutteridge brothers, Harry and Walter. Later both were promoted to sergeant. Harry Gutteridge wrote in his account of the retreat:

> Now bear in mind, the retreat had taken 13 days and with high explosives and the heavy guns massed against us, flanked by thousands, it was a glorious retreat of over 200 miles, and then to turn on the Marne and carry on without a stop until we were well established on the Aisne and had the French stood, or even retired with us, there would have been a different tale to tell, and the Aisne would not have been held by the enemy. The British rifle fire deadly and against the massed German troops quite upset their plan of destroying those two British Army Corps.

With their continuing advance, the German supply problems had worsened and they had no inkling that a counter-offensive was imminent. On 5 September the Battle of the Marne began. For the next eight days the Germans were driven back. Harry Gutteridge wrote: 'For a week on the Marne we turned and fought them back day and night, gaining 70 miles of ground, and then to get up 400 to 500 feet on to the Aisne.'

On the night of 12 September the opposing forces were within the Aisne area. On the afternoon of the next day the 2nd Battalion crossed the River Aisne by pontoon bridge constructed by the side of the broken bridge at Pont Arcy. Then to Soupier where they remained until the afternoon of 14 September, being shelled with both high explosives and shrapnel.

Major Eden wrote in his diary: 'The enemy's artillery fire was at times very heavy, and did us a great deal of damage. A and B companies were in the open, with firing line so situated that they could not use their rifles, and suffered several casualties. One H.E. shell, bursting at one spot, killed four men and wounded another four.'

A shell wounded Private William Mayne on that day, 14 September. One Stoke Poges soldier, probably Harry Gutteridge, in a letter home wrote: 'My chum, E. Elderfield, was with him in the same company when he was wounded, and told me how cheerful he was when they left the wood. Their company had 43 casualties that day.' William Mayne died of his wounds on 22 September 1914, leaving a widow and one child, the first man from Stoke Poges to give his life in the First World War. He is buried in St Nazaire (Toutes-Aides) Cemetery, Loire Atlantique, France, grave reference A18, a long way from where he was wounded. St Nazaire was used as a location for treating the wounded because of the uncertainty at that stage of the war of being able to hold the Channel ports.

Sidney Measday – Sunk Twice off Alexandria

Three Measday brothers, Frank, the eldest, Walter and Sidney, served in the war. Only Frank, who was wounded in 1916, survived. They lived in 2 Sefton Park Cottages with their mother Alice. All three boys were in the parish church choir.

Sidney, the youngest, born in 1893, was employed by Lord Decies, and had just come home to live when war broke out. He joined the South Irish Horse on 1 January 1915 and was later transferred to the 3rd Battalion of the Royal Dublin Fusiliers. He was probably in Ireland when the Easter Rebellion took place. The Parish Magazine records him with the rank of sergeant.

The Dublin Fusiliers were on their way to Egypt in December 1917 to provide reinforcements for the army operating in Palestine under General Allenby when the troop ship they were on, the *Aragon*, was torpedoed.

97 *Frank, Sidney and Walter with their mother Charlotte Alice Measday.*

The *Aragon*, a Royal Mail Steam Packet Company ship, conveyed the image of leisured Edwardian luxury when she entered service in 1905. She became a troopship in 1915. Arriving off Alexandria on 30 December 1917, she entered the harbour, but as there was no berth available she was ordered out again. She was to anchor outside where, unprotected, she was an easy target.

The *Aragon*, with 2,700 troops and nurses aboard her, was torpedoed by U boat *U34*.* Lady Harkness,† one of the nurses who survived, wrote a detailed account of the attack, a summary of which describes what happened.

The ship was turning in a circle to lessen the risk of torpedoes, with passengers on deck waiting for the ship to resume her course, and for the church service to start, the service was already late, it was five minutes past eleven on the morning of Sunday 30 December 1917, when the ship was hit by a torpedo.

The *Aragon* took 17½ minutes to disappear. In that time, following the calls to stations and abandon ship, she healed over, tilting the decks to an angle that made the lowering of the boats on that side extremely difficult.

Men jumped overboard‡ and the boats picked up as many survivors as they could. Overloaded boats in danger of capsizing had no option but to move off to avoid the suction caused by the sinking ship. Those still in the water were left but, fortunately, HMS *Attack*, the destroyer escort, moved in alongside the sinking *Aragon* and picked up survivors amongst whom was Sidney Measday.

U34 waited for the *Aragon* to disappear and then torpedoed the destroyer. Lady Harkness records the sinking:

> The most horrible part was yet to come. The men who had been picked up by the destroyer were stripping off their wet clothing and life-jackets, and one could imagine their relief at being hauled to safety.
>
> As we watched the spot where the *Aragon* had been, there was another terrific bang, and a high spout of water shot up from the middle of the destroyer, breaking her clean in two. There followed the deep roar of an underwater explosion, and we saw hundreds of men diving into the water.
>
> The two halves of our escort sank at once, leaving a rapidly spreading oil slick on the sea. The boats moved in at once in an attempt to rescue the survivors of the double sinking, but the men now without life-jackets, were so covered with oil that they were unable to hold on to the ropes that were thrown to them. Many were so sickened by the oil that they had swallowed that when their hands slipped from ours, they had no strength to swim and sank at once. I shall never forget their heart-rending cries.

---

* The *U34*, launched in May 1914, sank 121 ships, excluding warships. She last sailed on 18 October 1918 and was never heard from again.

† The Papers of Lady Harkness, held in the Department of Documents at the Imperial War Museum, reference 79/46/1. Lady Harkness, then Florence Margaret Furniss, was a nurse with Queen Alexandra's Imperial Military Nursing Service. She married Joseph Harkness in 1920 and he was knighted in 1956.

‡ Lady Harkness also recalled that one of the strictest rules on board was that life jackets should be carried at all times. They were cumbersome things in those days, made of large blocks of cork, and, if not properly adjusted, could cause the wearer serious injury should he have to jump from a height into the water.

98 *Left: This poster advertising Royal Mail services shows the* Aragon *steaming at full speed. (Courtesy: Southampton City Council Museums, Furness Withy Collection.)*

99 *Above: Sidney Measday.*

Sidney Measday was one of the 610 victims of this double tragedy and his body was washed up three days later and he was buried in Alexandria (Hadra) War Memorial Cemetery, grave reference G90.

On 16 February 1918, a few weeks later, a Court Martial was held into the loss of HMS *Attack* and the court finding was:

> The Commanding Officer of HMS *Attack* concluded erroneously that the *Aragon* had struck a mine; whereas it is fairly certain that she was torpedoed.
>
> Had he not made this mistake the *Attack* would presumably not remained stopped on the spot where *Aragon* was sunk. This mistake therefore contributed to the torpedoing of *Attack*, though it cannot be said that the destroyer would not have been torpedoed in the course of such life-saving measures, as the commanding officer would in any case have been bound to take.
>
> The error was however a perfectly natural one under the circumstances, i.e. mines reported in the close vicinity, and it is considered that no blame attaches to the commanding officer on this account.

The Commanding Officer who was exonerated was Lieut Harry Alexander Dukes Keate, R.N.

Walter Measday – Killed by a Sniper

100 *Walter Measday.*

Walter Measday, the middle of the three brothers, worked for the Howard-Vyse family and then moved to Folkestone. He joined the South Staffordshire Regiment in March 1916, serving as a private.

Only four months later Walter left for France where he remained until his death. He was killed on 1 July 1917, at the age of 26, near Lens but the exact location of his grave is unknown because the ground fought over was taken and retaken.

The 1/6th Battalion South Staffordshire War Diary records the events of that day:

> The Battalion took part in the attack on the western defences of LENS on the early morning of 1 July 1917. A coy. acted as carrying party for the 1/5 North Staffordshire Regt. B coy. acted as their moppers up. C and D coys. served as support to the same Regt. A coy. performed its task successfully and suffered heavy casualties losing all its officers. C and D coy. attained their support positions but were not called upon for active operations during the fight. B coy. was organised into four parties of 20 men, each party being attached to the leading platoon of the four companies of the 5th North Staffordshire Regt who formed the assaulting troops. Considerable opposition was encountered but two of the four companies reached their objective, ACONITE trench in the city of LENS but were isolated owing to the failure of the flank brigades to reach their objectives. Casualties were heavy and Lieut H.P. Jones B Coy found himself in charge of the remnants of two companies 5th North Staffords as well as his own men in the church square CITE DUMOULIN. He consolidated the square and disposed of his men in support of the two successful companies incidentally capturing 8 prisoners and 3 machine guns. In the early afternoon his party were heavily counter attacked from both flanks and forced to return to AGUE trench thus leaving the ACONITE parties isolated. The men in ACONITE were either killed or taken prisoners. At 6 p.m. orders were received from the O.C. 1/5 South Staffordshire Regt., who had taken over command of the Brigade forces, to withdraw to LIEVIN as a fresh assault was being launched at midnight.

His officer wrote to his mother:

> While taking part in an attack on the enemy trenches he was sniped and killed instantly. It will be some slight consolation to you to know that he

> suffered no pain. He was always prepared to do anything he could to help and to go anywhere, however dangerous. I personally feel his loss very keenly; as I am sure do all his comrades. We all feel the greatest sympathy with you in your great loss.

Walter is commemorated on bay 6 of the Arras Memorial, Pas de Calais, France. His eldest brother Frank survived.

The Parish Magazine reported in July 1915: All the men of Sefton Park Cottages who can are serving their country either at home or abroad. It has been suggested that these houses should be renamed "Patriotic Terrace".' There were eight men serving.

Henry Mitchell – East Surrey Regiment

Henry Frederick Mitchell was the son of Albert and Anne Mitchell of Hollybush Hill, Stoke Poges. Henry's father was a carpenter but we do not know Henry's occupation.

Towards the end of 1915 he volunteered for the 12th Battalion of the East Surrey Regiment and became a corporal. He was severely wounded in the groin by a bullet and transported to the General Hospital in Boulogne where he died on 25 April 1917, aged 27.

Henry was unmarried and his mother by this time was widowed. He is buried in Boulogne Eastern Cemetery, Pas de Calais, France, grave reference IV.C.28.

Harry Newns – A Regular who Re-enlisted

Harry Newns had served 18 years in the 2nd Battalion of the South Staffordshire Regiment before the war and had re-enlisted in September 1914. Born in Hollins, Brampton, Derbyshire, in 1875, both his parents, James and Virtue Newns, were born in Dinton, Buckinghamshire.

The 1881 census records that at that time he had a brother Charlie two years younger than him and two sisters, Esther nine years his senior and Mary five years his senior. The two girls were born in Haddenham in Buckinghamshire and the two boys were born after their parents moved to Derbyshire. Other children were born after 1881. Harry's Stoke Poges connection resulted from his marriage on 5 August 1913 to Emily Mary Didcock of Stoke Green.

Within a month of re-joining, Harry Newns was promoted to sergeant and saw action in France. He was wounded in September 1915 by a shrapnel splinter and was crushed by a falling parapet caused by shellfire. The following year he suffered from concussion through the bursting of a shell.

His brother Charlie was killed on 12 October 1916, aged 40, in the Battle of the Somme, serving with the Lancashire Fusiliers. At the time Harry wrote home:

> I am with my old Battalion now, the one in which I served so many years, there are a few, but unfortunately only a few, of the old faces left that I know. I am still in the best of health and sincerely hope it will last, for under our present circumstances such a great deal depends on our health. I don't think Mr. Censor will be so bad as to pull me up for saying that we are in the thick of the fun once more. Remember me to my enquiring friends.

A month after his brother was killed, Harry also lost his life following an action in which he was wounded and posted missing. The South Staffordshire Regiment War Diary describes this action:

> 12th November – the Battalion moved into assembly trenches south of SERRE and during the night formed up for attack. There was practically no hostile shelling and no casualties occurred during the process of forming up.
>
> 13th November – the Battalion successfully crossed the German front line and assaulted the second line wire, which was practically uncut. The battalions from the left division came across our front breaking up our formations. Re-organisation was rendered difficult by the heavy mist. Casualties among officers and other ranks were very heavy. …
>
> 14th November – the old defensive lines in MONK and LEC END were re-occupied … On the night of 13/14th many casualties were evacuated from the dugouts in MONK and DELAUNAY.

The Parish Magazine in the December 1916 issue reported that Harry formed one of an attacking party on 13 November and had not been heard of since and had been reported as missing. The hope was that he had been wounded and taken prisoner.

More months passed before his death was confirmed. One informant stated his belief that after an unsuccessful attack it was the sergeant who insisted on going out to rescue the wounded and was killed by a shell. Then after nine months of ceaseless anxiety and enquiry from every possible source of information, Mrs Newns received word from the War Office that her husband, reported missing on 13 November 1916, was killed between 13 and 15 November, and that his body was afterwards found and buried by the Rev. E. Campbell. The Parish Magazine reported, September 1917:

> As far as the sad, but very grand, story can be pieced together it quite fits in with what one knew of the Sergeant, who was a soldier to the backbone. One witness writes 'Sergt. Newns was last seen wounded in the head but still carrying on.' A later witness adds, 'The Sergeant was killed by a shell whilst bandaging up the wounded.' It was probably all part of the long drawn out fighting from November 13th to 15th.

The October 1917 Parish Magazine includes a short obituary:

> Sergeant H.Newns, whose gallant death we referred to in our September issue, served 12½ years in India and 4½ in South Africa. He comes of a military family. His brother was killed just before him, 12 October 1916; he had a nephew killed in 1915, another severely wounded, and eight are still serving. The Sergeant was an excellent shot, and in 1909 won the Gold Jewel for South Africa in the Army Championship.

Harry Newns died on Wednesday 15 November 1916, aged 42. He was buried in Serre Road Cemetery No 2, Somme, grave reference 1.K.13. He is also commemorated on the Didcock family gravestone in St Giles' Churchyard.

Arthur William Plumridge – 56th Machine Gun Corps

Arthur Plumridge, who was killed aged 20 on 1 November 1916, was typical of the young men who displayed such keenness and patriotism to volunteer to serve their country at the earliest opportunity.

The Plumridge family lived at 2 Farnham Road Cottages, now Templewood Lane. George Edward and Emily Plumridge (née Day) had a large family. Daisy was born in 1893, Percy the following year, Arthur in 1896, Louise in 1899, Alice in 1902, Bertie James in 1905 and William John in 1908. George, the father, was born in Hedgerley but the rest of the family members were born in Stoke Poges and educated at the local school.

Arthur, who since leaving school had worked for the Post Office, was described in the Parish Magazine as being 'anything but strong and having undergone several operations … nothing would satisfy him but to get to the front.'

101 *Arthur and his father George Edward Plumridge.*

102 *King Edward Street, Chalvey,* c.*1910.*

103 *Arthur Plumridge, far left, with three of his friends.*

104 *The Main Post Office in Slough.*

He volunteered and joined the Royal Bucks Hussars in July 1915. A letter written to him when he was in training by his sweetheart May, who lived in King Edward Street, Chalvey, and dated 24 July 1915, has survived. In it she expresses the great anxieties that mothers, wives and sweethearts must have felt as young men went to war. She refers to a mutual friend, Ted Speed, who she writes 'is sailing to France or some where abroad' continuing 'and he has only been enlisted 3 months.' She questions whether his three months' training was enough for the front. She reports:

> I also hear the troops are on the move everywhere now, so I guess there must be another big battle coming off very soon. It does seem wicked ducks having to lose such a lot of men. Well darling one I do hope the war will be over very soon, for I do not want you to go darling.

But Arthur did go to the front the following year. His brother Percy had joined the Oxford and Bucks Light Infantry at the beginning of the war and reached the rank of corporal. Although he was wounded three times, he survived.

At the time when Arthur was being trained in 1915 at the Machine Gun Training Centre at Grantham, the use of machine gun companies was being

VOLUME No. 10.

Instructions regarding War Diaries and Intelligence Summaries are contained in F. S. Regs., Part II. and the Staff Manual respectively. Title Pages will be prepared in manuscript.

WAR DIARY of 56 Machine Gun Coy. for NOVEMBER. 1916

~~INTELLIGENCE~~ SUMMARY

(Erase heading not required.)

Army Form C. 2118

Place	Date	Hour	Summary of Events and Information	Remarks and references to Appendices
AVELUY	1.11.16 ~~2.11.16~~		Intersection Relief. No 3 Sect & 2 guns of No 4 sect. relieved No 1 sect. & other 2 guns of No 4 sect. in front line. Trenches over the knees in mud & water. Casualties Pte Plumridge killed Sgt Brocklebank wounded Ptes. Lord, Barber, Clarke, Whiteside & Ball wounded. Trenches heavily shelled with shrapnel.	RWO
	2.11.16		Relief of front line guns by 58th M.G.C. Trenches again heavily shelled by shrapnel. Casualties. 2 Lt Price wounded. Ptes Keeble, Howes, Allday wounded	RWO
	3.11.16		No 2 Sect. at Thiepval. Sections 1, 3 & 4 cleaning guns & equipment.	RWO
	4.11.16		No 4 Sect relieved No 2 Sect at Thiepval. Sections Nos 1, 2, & 3 had baths at Aveluy	RWO
	5.11.16		Coy relieved 58 Coy in front line. Coy H.Q moved from AVELUY WOOD to X2a 5.6. No 1 Sect. 4 guns in front line. No 3 Sect. 4 guns in front line. No 2 Sect 2 guns in support line 1 gun CHQ 1 gun deficient. No 4 Sect 2 guns in support line 2 guns at Thiepval. Relief complete by 6.30 pm.	
	6.11.16		No change 2 teams of No 2 sect. took rations up to Hessian.	RWO
	7.11.16		Intersection relief. No 2 Sect relieved No 3 sect in front line. No 4 Sect. relieved No 1 Sect in front line. Trenches in bad condition. Communication trenches impassable. Casualties Cpl Gordon killed Pte Young wounded	RWO
	8.11.16		Coy relief by 57th M.G.C. Coy moved into billets in AVELUY. Casualties Pte Nutt killed Pte Leslie wounded 2 Lt Oakes joined Coy from Camiers.	RWO
	9.11.16		Coy cleaned guns. Rifle & gun inspection by Sect. Officers. 2 Lt Cooper joined Coy from Camiers	RWO
	10.11.16		Coy inspection. Gun drill. Belt filling. Kit & clothing inspection	RWO
	11.11.16		Coy drill. Rifle inspection. Belt filling & advanced drill.	RWO
	12.11.16		Sections Nos 1 & 2 and 2 teams of No 4 section relieved [illegible] Coy in front line. No 3 section & ½ No 4 section in reserve at AVELUY. O.C. Coy moved his H.Q. to Stuff Trench	RWO

1875 Wt. W593/826 1,000,000 4/15 J.B.C. & A. A.D.S.S./Forms/C. 2118.

105 *The War Diary entry for 56th Machine Gun Company recording the death of Arthur Plumridge.*

reviewed. The machine gun was one of the most deadly weapons in use. The new Vickers gun was replacing the old Maxim gun. Fired from a tripod, cooled by water held in a jacket against the barrel, the bullets were assembled in a canvas belt, which held 250 rounds and lasted 30 seconds at the maximum rate of fire. Two men carried the equipment – the tripod and gun weighed 28.5 and 20 pounds respectively – two carried the ammunition and there were two spare men.

In October 1915 when the Machine Gun Corps was created, each company took its number from the Infantry Brigade to which it was attached. Just over a third of those who served in the MGC became casualties. The enemy's concern was always to knock out the machine guns that took so many lives on both sides. It is no surprise that the MGC was known as the Suicide Club.

Arthur Plumridge transferred to the 56th Machine Gun Corps, 19th (Western) Division and three months after fighting at the front he was killed in Stuff Trench,* part of the Somme battlefield, where the 56th Brigade was heavily engaged.

His mother received two letters from the front, one from his officer and another from his chum. His officer wrote:

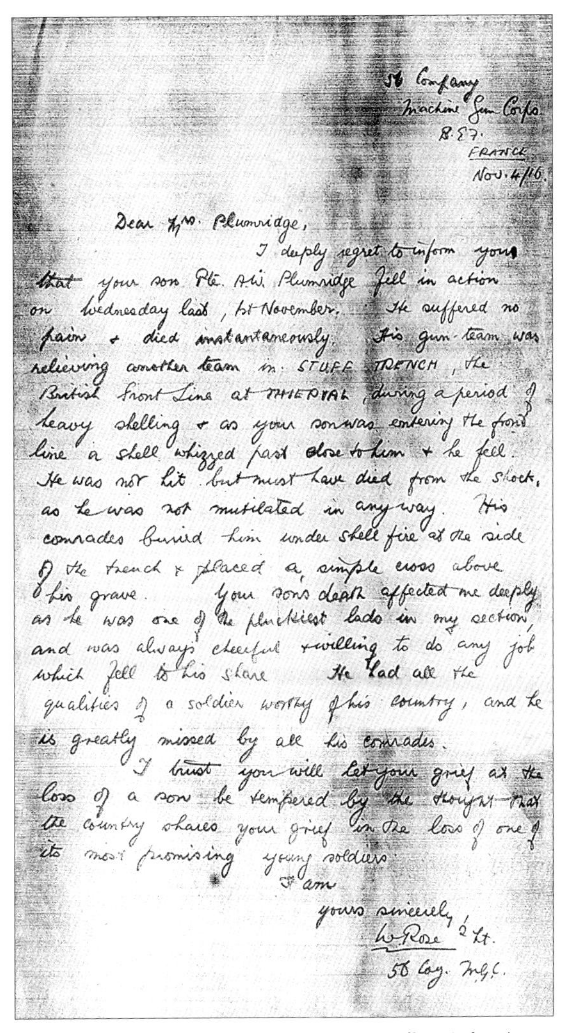
56 Company
Machine Gun Corps
B.E.F.
FRANCE
Nov. 4/16.

Dear Mrs. Plumridge,
I deeply regret to inform you that your son Pte. A.W. Plumridge fell in action on Wednesday last, 1st November. He suffered no pain & died instantaneously. His gun-team was relieving another team in STUFF TRENCH, the British Front Line at THIEPVAL, during a period of heavy shelling & as your son was entering the front line a shell whizzed past close to him & he fell. He was not hit but must have died from the shock, as he was not mutilated in any way. His comrades buried him under shell fire at the side of the trench & placed a simple cross above his grave. Your son's death affected me deeply as he was one of the pluckiest lads in my section, and was always cheerful & willing to do any job which fell to his share. He had all the qualities of a soldier worthy of his country, and he is greatly missed by all his comrades.
I trust you will let your grief at the loss of a son be tempered by the thought that the country shares your grief in the loss of one of its most promising young soldiers.
I am
yours sincerely,
W. Rose 2 Lt.
56 Coy. M.G.C.

106 *The letter from Arthur Plumridge's officer informing his mother of the death of her son.*

> He suffered no pain and died instantaneously. His gun team was relieving another team in STUFF TRENCH, the British front line at Thiepval, during a period of heavy shelling and as your son was entering the front line a shell whizzed past close to him and he fell. He was not hit but must have died from the shock, as he was not mutilated in any way. His comrades buried him under shellfire at the side of the trench and placed a simple cross above his grave. Your son's death affected me deeply as he was one of the pluckiest lads in my section, and always cheerful and willing to do any job which fell to his share. He had all the qualities of a soldier worthy of his country.

---

* Stuff Trench was to the north of Thiepval. It had been captured ten days before in an assault on 21 and 22 October 1916 in which the poet Edmund Blunden was involved.

His chum also wrote and described Arthur's death from the bursting of the shell in the trench where he was sitting:

> I felt it very much as he was my best chum. We came out of the same regiment and went to Grantham and came out here together and we had been together all the time till this last week when I was put on another gun team for a bit and he had just come to relieve us when he was hit.

After the war, Arthur was re-buried in Connaught Cemetery, Thiepval, Somme, grave reference IX.J.5.

James Pullen – Team Driver, Royal Field Artillery

James Henry Pullen was born on 3 March 1885, the son of James and Louisa Pullen. His father was a carman and the family lived in Battersea. In the 1891 census we find James, then six, living with his grandparents in Rickmans Hill, Stoke Poges. It seems probable that his mother died when he was quite young and his grandmother, Mary Pullen, cared for him.

The 1901 census reveals that his father was still living in London in St Pancras. James was still living with his grandparents in Rickmans Hill. He was now 16 and at work as a carter on a farm dealing with horses. Later the family moved to Gladstone Cottages in Rogers Lane. He attended the local school.

James enlisted in the Royal Field Artillery in September 1915 as a driver of a gun team. The Parish Magazine, October 1915 issue, included his name as one of those who had joined up. It also included a paragraph:

> Mrs Pullen, West End, whose grandson's name appears in this month's list, has 12 grandsons – six of whom are brothers, five soldiers and one sailor – serving their Country. Four of her grandchildren are in Canadian Regiments, and two others are serving in France.

In May 1917 James wrote home:

> I have now been 17 months in France, which country takes the biscuit for rough winters, but it is lovely in summer. I have now been away from the D.A.C.* six months. Falling sick I was sent to hospital for a month, and on leaving was put into a battery. I lost my Christmas parcel through being in hospital.

However, the next Christmas, 1917, he did receive his parcel. Four months later, on 29 April 1918, James Pullen was killed by a shell and the Parish Magazine reported yet another sad death:

> Driver J.H. Pullen, who lived with his grandmother in Gladstone Cottages, has been killed in action. His relations have our heartfelt sympathy. He was struck by a shell on 30 April,† and passed away without suffering and was buried in the military cemetery. As a boy he was in the

---

* D.A.C. Divisional Ammunition Column.

† The Commonwealth War Graves Commission record the date of death as 29 April 1918.

> Parish Church choir, and since was in the employ of Mr. Burt and Lord Decies. He had been two years in France and three in the army. His comrades write that he was much respected in the battery.

In the next issue the letter from his Major to his grandmother was printed:

> He was one of my best and most trusted drivers. He was driving one of my gun teams, a most honoured post. The best men and horses always make these teams, as they are the men who get the gun out of difficulties on the move – the first in action and the last out. He had been doing excellent work during the recent troublous times, and was killed by a shell whilst his team was close up to the guns in action ...

107 *The grave of James Pullen.*

James Pullen was 33 when he died and is buried in Acheux Military Cemetery, Somme, France, grave reference plot 1, row C, grave 14. At the foot of his headstone are the words 'GONE BUT NEVER FORGOTTEN BY HIS LOVING GRANDMOTHER MARY PULLEN'. Mary Pullen moved to Temple Cottage and died the following year aged 87.

Francis Joseph Reynolds – Grenadier Guardsman

Francis Joseph Reynolds was a 19-year-old footman from Enstone, near Woodstock, in Oxfordshire, when he volunteered for the Grenadier Guards in March 1901. Described as 5ft 6in tall, with fresh complexion and flaxen hair, blue eyes and weighing 137 lbs. He signed on to serve three years with the Colours and nine years on the Reserve.

He left the Grenadier Guards in 1904 and three years later married Alice Arthur also from Enstone. A year later their first child Kitty was born and they had three other children, John, Tracey, and Francis who was born in October 1914 in Stoke Poges.

Sometime after 1908 the couple moved to Stoke Poges where Frank, as he was known, became one of the local postmen. Frank was called up as a reservist at the beginning of the war, but was rejected because of varicose veins. He underwent an operation and was passed for home service. The Parish Magazine recorded that 'stirred up by the sight of men, who had been wounded, going out for a second time, when he had not been out at all, he persuaded the doctor to pass him for the front, though still far from cured.'

He was posted to the front in August 1915 but died of wounds on 21 April 1916. The 3rd Battalion had been in Ypres until 4 April and after a rest returned to the same trenches on 7 April which the Battalion Diary recorded 'was worse than ever owing to the Scots Guards having been subjected to another severe bombardment'.

The Battalion Diary records the events of 19 to 24 April. On 19 April the Battalion had moved into support in Ypres. One company was in the Prison, which had been shelled on 21 April. Since Frank Reynolds was hit by a shell fragment that day, it is likely he was in the Prison. The diary also stated that all men had been issued with steel helmets.

Corporal Reynolds was taken to a dressing station and the chaplain wrote to Mrs Reynolds:

108 *Edward Nathaniel Cook and his wife. Mr Cook was the sub-postmaster until he retired in 1925.*

> I got to the dressing room where he had been taken when hit by a shell, and finding him unconscious (he was just passing away) I committed his soul to God. All that could be done for him had been done by doctor and comrades. This was on Good Friday. It was my sad duty to lay his body to rest on Easter Eve and after the service some of his comrades came to talk to me and to tell me how much he was thought of and respected in his platoon. We all thought of him on Easter Day when we were giving God thanks for the resurrection from the dead.

109 *The Stoke Poges Post Office in Uxbridge Road, built 1912, where Mr Cook was the sub-postmaster.*

His sergeant also wrote:

> He was struck by a fragment of shell and died very soon afterwards from the shock. We regret his death because he was so well liked and such a good man. He is buried some distance behind the firing line and accorded full military honours.

Francis Joseph Reynolds, who died aged 34, is buried in Ypres Reservoir Cemetery, Ieper, West Vlaanderen, Belgium, grave reference I.C.49.

In March 1917 the Parish Magazine reported that Mrs Reynolds was moving with her children to Oxfordshire to be near the grandparents on both sides. This, they felt, was a wise decision. Two months later Mrs Reynolds wrote from Rectory Farm, Church Enstone, to thank all those who had subscribed towards the cost of the removal. Mr Cook, at the Post Office, had collected over £11 as a slight token of regard for one of the village postmen.

Charles Robinson – One of Hartley's Men

Charles John Robinson, who volunteered early in 1915, was killed almost at the end of the war on 16 October 1918, aged 26.

The son of James Robinson, a bricklayer, and his wife Emily, he was born in Stoke Poges and worked for Hartley's, the local builder. His wife Violet Annie Robinson's address was given as The Hut, Rogers Lane, but prior to his death he was listed on the 1918 Electoral Roll as an absent voter with the address of Rose Cottage, School Lane.

Charles served initially as a private in the Oxford and Bucks Light Infantry and subsequently in the 36th Battalion Machine Gun Company. In October 1918 he was serving in Belgium where the 36th Battalion MGC War Diary records the events of that month. On the 7th his company moved to Reutel and rested there until the 13th, refitting and preparing for action. On the night of the 13th:

> A and B companies moved up with the 107th and 109th Brigades which attacked on the right and left respectively at 05.35 14th, in the direction of KEZELBERG, MOORSEELE, GUILLEGPEM and HEULE. The advance reached just west of MOORSEELE on this day, but was checked. Guns of both A and B Companies worked well forward in close support of the attack, and engaged targets with direct observation.

The diary continued with an entry for the 15th and 16th:

> The advance was resumed on the 15th. MOORSEELE, GULLEGHEM and HEULE were captured. B Company engaged enemy machine guns, which were checking the advance and materially assisted the capture of HEULE by supporting fire. Battalion HQ moved to BAKEWELL FARM, DADIZEELE, and advanced Battalion HQ with advanced Division HQ to ASHMORE FARM. During the night 15th – 16th the 108th Brigade with C Company attached passed through A and B Companies (which remained in position) and continued the advance on the 16th, reaching the line of the LYS.

Charles Robinson was severely wounded on 16 October and died shortly after reaching the dressing station. He is buried in Cement House Cemetery, Langemarck, in Belgium, grave reference XVII.D.8. The Commonwealth War Graves Commission records that among those re-interred in this cemetery were the graves of six British soldiers buried in Heule Churchyard in October 1918.

Walter Rogers – Died of Wounds on the Somme

Walter Rogers, whose father was a shepherd, was born in Denham as was his brother Leonard. Both brothers worked for Captain Bell-White of Alderbourne Manor. Their parents Harry and Elizabeth Rogers resided at Gate House, Fulmer Grange, within the parish of Stoke Poges.

Walter was a lance-corporal with the 9th Battalion of the Royal Fusiliers. He was wounded whilst fighting on the Somme Battlefield in October 1916. The Regimental Diary of the 9th Royal Fusiliers records the events of those few days before he died of his wounds:

> October 6th, Trenches West of Gueudecourt – Hostile shelling very heavy all day on front and support trenches and on Sunken Road also FLERS. Casualties sustained not quite so heavy as usual, 2/Lt. Bird wounded. At 11.30 a.m. and 12.45 p.m. two hostile aeroplanes came over lines, flying very low about 200 ft. up. M.G.s opened fire and sent them back. Orders received for tomorrow's resumed offensive. 2nd Lieut Edwards went down with shell shock. Systematic bombardment of enemy's line by our artillery began at 7.15 p.m. and continued up to ZERO.
>
> October 7th – Zero at 1.45 p.m. 8th R.F and 9th RF attacking, 7th Sussex in support, 11th Middlesex in Reserve. 37th Bde. attacking on our Right, – 35th Bde. in Divl. Reserve. A, B and D Companies took up their position in the advanced trench in front of GIRD SUPPORT overnight, with C Coy. in GIRD SUPPORT TRENCH as the supporting company, D = Right Coy. B= Centre Coy. A=Left Coy. Coys. went over in two lines – also the supporting Coy. – which rushed over from GIRD SUPPORT to the Advanced trench immediately the attacking Coys. went forward. Contrary to expectations, very heavy m gun and rifle fire was encountered immediately the first line reached the top of the ridge also very heavy shelling. The three front Coys. and two platoons of the supporting Company were practically decimated by this fire. B Coy. apparently swung out to their right to get into touch with A Coy. and were enfiladed by 2 MGs. The first objective was not reached by any Company. Enemy were observed to take in some of our wounded of B and D Coys. A body of Germans also commenced to advance on our left, but were driven back by our MG fire, which was immediately opened upon them. Some stragglers crawled back at dusk, and we continued to hold our original front line, with these men and the two remaining platoons of C Coy. The artillery barrage had been a creeping one, and apparently had missed the first German trench, which was nearer than it appeared. Our barrage remained for some time behind our second objective, until it was known that the attack had failed. A similar result accrued from the attack on our left and right.

> Up to the time of going over the top our casualties had been Officers – 8, O.Ranks 109 and 20 sick, so the Battn. was rather weak on going over. In the attack the losses were
>
> | | Officers | O Ranks |
> |---|---|---|
> | Killed | 4 | 21 |
> | Wounded | 1 | 131 |
> | Missing | 4 | 161 |
> | Total | 9 | 313 |
>
> In a personal note to the Commanding Officer the G.O.C. 36th Infy Bde said: – 'Will you please thank all ranks of your Battn. for the magnificent gallantry they displayed yesterday. They advanced steadily under a very heavy fire, which only the very best troops could have faced. Although unfortunately unsuccessful your gallant conduct has added to the fine reputation which you have already won for yourselves.'
>
> The Battn was relieved by the 11th M'x (2 Companies), the other 2 Coys. of the 11th M'x relieving the 8th RF on our left. The 7th Sussex moved up in support.

Walter Rogers was wounded in this action and taken to the 36th Casualty Clearing Station at Heilly where he died on 9 October 1916, aged 22. He is buried in Heilly Station Cemetery, Mericourt-L'Abbe, Somme, grave reference III. D. 65.

Walter was unmarried and his employer, Captain Bell-White, wrote this tribute in the Parish Magazine:

> Walter Rogers was under gardener here, and was one of the first to volunteer to join the Army at the outbreak of war. We are all very sorry to hear of his death. He was an excellent workman, and to mark my appreciation of his sense of duty, I allowed him half his wages whilst on Active Service, and promised to keep his situation open for him if he returned. His brother also worked for me, and being a reservist, he was called up at once, and is now a prisoner in Germany. The parents have our sincere sympathy, and it must be a comfort and satisfaction to them to know that their sons have so nobly done their duty.

Edwin Shepherd – An Explosion Sinks the *Vanguard*

Edwin Shepherd joined the Royal Navy at the age of 14, the year before the outbreak of the First World War. He was born in Broughton, Hampshire, but his family lived in Sandhurst during his school years.

He attended St Michael's C of E School, Sandhurst, until he was fourteen. He gained many prizes both at the Sunday and day schools, including the Bishop of Oxford's Prize for Scripture. He was in the St Michael and All Angels Church Choir and was the solo singer for the three years before he left.

Whilst he was in the Navy his parents, Ernest and Agnes Shepherd, moved to Stoke Poges. Ernest was a gardener and the family's Stoke Poges address of Lion Lodge suggests that he was employed at Stoke Park, perhaps on the golf course.

110 *HMS* Vanguard.

111 *The entrance lodges to Stoke Park, c.1911. The Shepherd family lived in the one on the left and the Skues family in the one on the right.*

Edwin's service records give his height as 5ft 6½in, chest 34, dark brown hair, grey eyes and fresh complexion. At the age of 14 he joined a training ship and was then transferred to the Royal Navy for wireless telegraphy and gained a naval grant of £25. The picture that emerges from his service records is that he was a conscientious and hard working boy sailor.

He served in HMS *Powerful, Impregnable, Vernon* and *Vanguard*. Edwin joined the *Vanguard* in March 1915. At the Battle of Jutland (31 May/1 June 1916) he was recommended for early promotion. He was given a man's rating at 17½ as ordinary telegraphist and, on his 18th birthday, 30 April 1917, was rated a telegraphist. A keen churchman and regular communicant, he was a member of the chaplain's bible class on the *Vanguard*.

Edwin Shepherd died when HMS *Vanguard* was destroyed by an internal explosion at 11.20 p.m. on 9 July 1917, when lying in Scapa Flow. She blew up with the loss of 804 sailors, with only three survivors, one of whom died later of his wounds.

In *British Battleships 1892-1957*, Randolph Pears wrote that the explosion 'rocked the next ship in line, *Collingwood*, and lit up the whole sky with its glare. In three minutes she had disappeared, leaving behind her an immense column of smoke ...'*

Midshipman H.C.Burton was asleep in his hammock in HMS *Warspite* and he wrote in his First World War Diary:

> I jumped out and ran to the Quarter Deck. A sight never to be forgotten met my eyes. No sign of the stricken ship was to be seen, but on all sides and from every direction, searchlights were being played on the spot where she went down. Boats of every description were already making their way to the empty billet. High in the air was a vast column of smoke drifting steadily towards Flotta. ... We were told to patrol near Flotta, which we did for about an hour and a half. The water was thick with oil fuel and cushions and other wreckage was floating everywhere. All around were trolling boats and picket boats seeking for survivors and corpses.†

The force of the explosion was such that a packet of pound notes from the ship's safe fell outside a crofter's cottage on Flotta Island a mile away. Midshipman Brian de Courcy-Ireland has written:

> As for me, I was one of those who walked along that dreadful mile of beach on Flotta with buckets. I will leave the description of it to Rudyard Kipling who, in his poem *The Scholars* referring to us, wrote:
> 'They have touched a knowledge outreaching speech – as when the cutters were sent
> To harvest the dreadful mile of beach after the *Vanguard* went.'
> I believe our sickberth staff pieced together over a score of bodies.

A Court of Inquiry considered that the explosion might have been caused by spontaneous detonation of cordite, which had become unstable, or by the cordite having caught fire from heating in an adjacent compartment or by sabotage. Sabotage was considered the least likely. During the First World War 11 battleships and large cruisers, from four navies, were destroyed by internal explosions when lying in harbour, possibly from deterioration of the stocks of high explosive on board.‡

There was much sorrow at the death of the 18-year-old Edwin Shepherd. The Stoke Poges Parish Magazine reported 'Canon Parsons, the Rector of Sandhurst, said from the pulpit how deeply he felt Shepherd's death, and that he had never come across a lad who did his duty to God and men more satisfactorily.' Mr G.C.Oldham, headmaster of his old school, wrote of him as 'one of the best it was my privilege to teach ... I have lost a friend in Edwin.' He is commemorated on the Portsmouth Naval Memorial, on Southsea Common, panel number 25, and on a Memorial Plaque in St Michael and All Angels Church, Sandhurst.

---

* Pears, Randolph, *British Battleships, 1892-1957* (1957).

† The Papers of Commander H.C.Burton RN, Extracts from The First World War Diary of Midshipman H.C.Burton, held in the Department of Documents at the Imperial War Museum, reference 81/31/1.

‡ Arthur, Max, *The True Glory, The Royal Navy: 1914-1939, A Narrative History* (1996).

Harold Skues – The Attack on Delville Wood

The Skues family were living in Denham when Harold was born in 1887. His father was a gamekeeper and then a gardener's labourer. The family moved to Stoke Poges to live at North Lodge, Stoke Park. At the outbreak of war Harold, who was unmarried, had worked at Stoke Park for 14 years since leaving Stoke Poges School. He lived with his parents. It is probable that his father also worked at Stoke Park, by then a golf course.

Harold joined the Oxford and Bucks Light Infantry in June 1915 and served in the 5th Battalion. He went to the front in October of that year where his battalion was part of 42nd Brigade, 14th Light Division.

Extracts from two of his letters home were published in the Parish Magazine. In a letter dated 17 December he wrote: 'We are sleeping in barns, back from the firing line, which is such a treat after the trenches, one gets very tired of mud and water.'

Two months later, February 1916, he wrote:

> We have had our share of shells round this district we have occupied, which, no doubt, you know, is one of the main roads the German wanted, but they will never be able to push the boys back now. These rifles are very true, used by cool men.
>
> The sights here are very dismal – nothing but broken-down houses and trees in all directions: and shell holes, which are so unpleasant to fall into at night – for we move at night. One walks along quite

112 *Digging a communication trench in Delville Wood. IWM photograph.*

> cheerfully, thinking he is very lucky only to be wet to the waist, because sometimes it is a long pull to free one from the mud, and often boots have to be left in the mud, and then you find all your buttons missing through your thigh boots having been tied to them.

The Battle of the Somme, the great offensive of 1916, commenced on 1 July 1916 and lasted for four and a half months. Five battalions of the Regiment took part at various times in the battle. It was during the second stage of the battle, lasting from 14 July to 13 September, that Delville Wood was the scene of fierce fighting as it was taken, retaken and part occupied. The clearing of Delville Wood had defeated no fewer than five other divisions until the 14th Division, of which the 5th Battalion Oxford and Bucks Light Infantry was part, achieved this task on 24 August.

Lieut S.R. Sebastian, in an account published in the Regimental Chronicle, described this action in which Corporal Harold Skues was killed on 24 August 1916:

> Two hours before the time for attack, which was 5.45 p.m., the heavy artillery opened. It turned the wood into a perfect hell. I saw the beginning of it. Trees were flying about like matches, and great columns of earth were thrown up

His report continued with a detailed account of the action, which was successful, but at a cost with three officers killed and seven wounded and with 42 other ranks killed, 111 wounded and seven missing.

Like so many others killed on the Somme, Corporal Harold Searle Skues, who was 28, is commemorated on the Thiepval Memorial, Somme, France, pier and face 10A and 10D. His father, whose only son he was, died a year later aged 69 and is buried in Stoke Poges Churchyard.

Ralph Stahr – Wounded and Missing in the Battle of Loos

We know little about Ralph Stahr except that he was a ward of Mrs E. Sayers of 3 Marshall's Cottages, Stoke Common. She apparently brought him up. In 1879 Rafael Henry Stahr, a hairdresser, married Lilian Violet Simmonds at St Pancras, London. Rafael's origins were Austrian and his wife Lilian was born in Ramsgate. They had a son, born towards the end of 1881, and named him Rafael Corie. Our Ralph Stahr's birth is given as 1883, just over a year later than Rafael. It is possible that he is the Rafael born in 1881 and that his Christian name became anglicised. There are no records of a Ralph Stahr being born in 1882, 1883, or 1884.

Ralph Stahr joined the 10th Battalion of the Gloucestershire Regiment early in the war. In August 1916, some eight months after he was killed, the Parish Magazine reported conflicting information about his death. It was reported that he was missing and last seen badly wounded at Hulluch, Loos. He died on 13 October 1915 at the Battle of Loos and his body was not recovered.

The Battle of Loos lasted from 25 September to 14 October 1915. This was the first battle in which the British used poison gas and the death toll exceeded in intensity that of any previous battle. The enemy used machine-guns to deadly effect and whole battalions were annihilated.

The entries in the War Diary of the 10th Battalion of the Gloucestershire Regiment for 7 to 13 October record the action in which Ralph Stahr went missing. On 11 October the Battalion moved into its battle position having in the previous few days worked to deepen, improve and dig new support and communication trenches.

On 12 October four companies took up positions, two in the firing line and two in support. The next day final preparations were made for the attack with the issue of bombs etc. The Diary records:

> The Battalion was ordered to attack German firing line just west of the LENS-LA BASSEE road between H.13 a 4.2 and H.13 a 4.7. After a preliminary artillery bombardment and gas attack the two companies in the firing line attacked punctually at 2 p.m. in two lines of two platoons each, the two companies in support moving out simultaneously into the British firing line. The attacking companies were led by Lt. L.W. Hastie and the support companies were in charge of Lt. W.S.Gange.

The battalion failed to reach its objective owing to heavy rifle and machine-gun fire from the enemy trenches and at nightfall was compelled to fall back on the original line.

In addition to two officers missing believed killed and three officers wounded, 150 other ranks were killed, wounded and missing. One of the missing, presumed killed in action on 13 October 1915, was Private Ralph Stahr. He was 32 years of age and unmarried and is commemorated on the Loos Memorial, Pas de Calais, panel 60 to 64.

Thomas Trinder – The Village Baker

Thomas Trinder was born 26 February 1887 at Stanton Harcourt in Oxfordshire. The 1901 Census reveals that he was then 14 years of age and living in Village Street, Stanton Harcourt with a baker called John Akers. Since his mother was Elizabeth Akers before she married his father George Trinder, John Akers could have been his uncle.

Thomas is listed in the census record as a servant and a baker's assistant and bread maker. His brother, William, aged 12, is also listed at the same address as a baker's assistant.

By 1910 Thomas, then 23, had arrived in Stoke Poges where he married the 18-year-old Charlotte Ware from Wexham Street towards the end of that year. Mr Newell, whose shop was on Bells Hill, employed him as a baker. The Trinders had four sons: George born 1912, Reginald born 1913, Phillip and Robert born 1916.

In October 1915 Thomas joined the Royal Marine Light Infantry as a baker giving his religion as Wesleyan. He was 5ft 9in tall. Two of his brothers served in the Royal Navy, another in the Army and a fourth joined up in July 1917.

In February 1917 he was sent to France and he died two months later on 28 April. He was killed at the Battle of Arras. One of the steps in this battle was the assault on the village of Gavrelle by the 189th and 190th Brigades of 63rd (Royal Naval) Division. The capture of the village by the 189th Brigade created a salient in the German lines but any further advance was inhibited because high ground to the north-east of the village where a windmill stood was still in German hands.

The War Diaries of the 1st and 2nd Battalions of the Royal Marine Light Infantry describe the attack to capture Gavrelle Windmill:

> 28th April 1917
>
> 4.25 a.m. Bn attacked in four waves the enemy trenches NE of Gavrelle with one platoon under 2nd Lieut. Newling detached to take Windmill. The Windmill on the left of the bt. front was reached & held but as 1st bt. RMLI on our left and 2nd Division on their left were hung up apparently by wire and owing to a large number of MGs, casualties were heavy.

The 1st Battalion moved into the jumping-off trenches on the previous evening and a patrol found the enemy wire uncut and strong. There were also casualties from shelling. The attack at 4.25 a.m. the next day in four waves was

113 *Advertisements in the Parish Magazine for local traders including Horace Newell, one of the two village bakers, who employed Thomas Trinder.*

114 *Left: Thomas Trinder.*

115 *Above: Charlotte Trinder and her four sons: George born 1912, Reginald born 1913, Philip year of birth not known and who died in infancy, and Robert born 1916.*

led by B Company. Thomas Trinder was in D Company on the right hand side of the attack behind B Company. Although the first two waves got to their objective they suffered from a massive enemy counter-attack and this led to fierce hand-to-hand fighting.

'The Royal Marines suffered 846 casualties of which 335 were dead, the worst losses in one day ever suffered by the Royal Marines.'*

The Parish Magazine reported Thomas Trinder's death:

> Private Trinder had lived here for 6½ years, and for 6 years had been in the employ of Mr. Newell, where he gained the respect and goodwill of all the customers and the entire confidence of Mr. Newell himself. And now by his sacrifice he has placed us all in his debt.

Thomas was reported to be missing but subsequently it was confirmed that he was 'killed in action previously reported missing'. A Red Cross enquiry for July 1917 established his place of burial. The 1st Battalion, Honourable Artillery Company, took the ground just to the north-west of the Mill, where he died, and his body was recovered.

Thomas Trinder is buried in Albuera Cemetery, Bailleul-sir-Berthoult, Pas de Calais, France, grave reference A.12. The village of Bailleul-sir-Berthoult is eight kilometres north-east of Arras.

* Tallet, Kyle, 'The Royal Marines at the Gavrelle Windmill 28th April 1917 – Triumph or Tragedy?', *Kyle Tallet Website*.

Within a year or so of her husband's death, Charlotte moved to Brighton. She was married for a second time on 29 July 1919 to Thomas Bean Nelson, a private in the Machine Gun Corps stationed at Maresfield Park Camp near Brighton.

Archibald McKechnie Tyson, MM – Ambulance Driver

We know little about Archibald McKechnie Tyson's Stoke Poges connections except that he came here after the end of the war, died of his wounds in January 1920, aged 29 years, and that he is buried here.

He joined the army in October 1915 and became an ambulance driver. In December 1917 he was awarded the Military Medal. Later, in March 1918, he met with an accident when he fell from the top of his ambulance whilst conveying wounded from the field dressing station near Bapaume, in France. This was three days after the Germans launched their great offensive and crossed the Somme and the day before they captured Bapaume. Tyson's injuries led to his discharge and the award of a pension but as a result he continued to suffer pain in his back.

Archibald Tyson married Margaret Ann Ferguson in Wandsworth, London, early in 1916 and they had a son at the end of that year who was named John F. Tyson.

They came to Stoke Poges, probably in 1920, and lived in Rough Hey Cottage at a time when Sir Edward Hugh Bray, who had been director of contracts in India with the rank of brigadier-general, lived in Rough Hey. Archibald Tyson was described on his death certificate as a chauffeur and may well have been employed in this capacity by Sir Edward Hugh Bray.

116 *Mr Kenneth Ross, Deputy Lieutenant, Buckinghamshire, having laid his wreath inscribed 'In Remembrance of Archibald Tyson and his service to his country', stands before the grave at the service of commemoration conducted by the Reverend Harry Latham. (Photograph by Phil Mills.)*

117 *Corporal Phillip Young, Royal Logistics Corps, successor to the Army Service Corps, sounds the Last Post during the service for Tyson. (Photograph by Phil Mills.)*

His death certificate also records that he died of severe wounds received during the war and that he had been gassed. Private Tyson is buried in St Giles' Churchyard but it was difficult to read the inscription on the grave. In 2003 the Commonwealth War Graves Commission, having received documents of his military service and medical history, passed them to the Ministry of Defence and it was confirmed that Archibald Tyson's grave would be treated as a war grave.

Archibald McKechnie Tyson is now properly recognised and a Commonwealth War Graves Commission headstone was erected over his grave in September 2005. A service of commemoration was held in St Giles' Churchyard on 29 October 2005.

Charles Wakefield – A Regular Soldier

Charles Wakefield died in 1920 of cerebral malaria in Dar es Salaam, in what was formerly German East Africa. Although he is buried in Dar es Salaam Cemetery, he also has a fine memorial, including a beautifully carved stone sword, in St Giles' Churchyard.

In 1896, at the age of 18, young Charles joined the Royal Irish Rifles. At this time his family lived in Rowlands Cottage, Bells Hill. His father, a saddler and harness maker and also called Charles, was a member of the newly created Parish Council. Charles questioned the way the parish charities were being run. He took issue with the church on which of the books and documents in the parish chest should be handed over to the new parish council.

Charles junior was also a determined individual and was keen on everything he undertook. A year after he joined the army he was posted to Ladysmith, South Africa, and two years later, seven months before the outbreak of the Boer War in October 1899, to India. In 1905 he won the Gold Jewel of India as a rifle shot and later, in 1913, came third in the Army Sixty at Bisley. During his time in India Charles learned Hindustani sufficiently well to be able to teach in the local Sunday schools. He was also a keen worker for the Royal Army Temperance Association and the YMCA.

In 1907, having returned from serving seven years in India, Charles married Abigail Howse. They had two children, first a girl Abigail, and then a boy Charles, both named after their parents.

Immediately on the outbreak of the First World War, and by now a quartermaster sergeant, he was posted to the Western Front. In November 1914 he was commissioned 'In the Field' as a second lieutenant, being promoted lieutenant the following March.

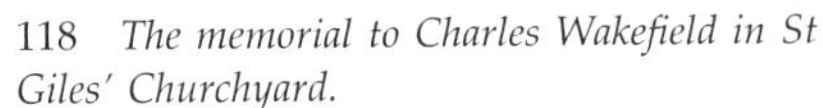

118 *The memorial to Charles Wakefield in St Giles' Churchyard.*

119 *Charles and Abigail Wakefield on their wedding day in 1907.*

In September 1915, now an acting captain, Wakefield was severely wounded. He spent part of his convalescence studying and qualifying in military sanitation. He was promoted captain in January 1917.

In June 1917 he wrote home describing an action in which the Royal Irish Rifles took part:

> Wednesday, June 16th, was a great day for the 2nd Battalion of the Royal Irish Rifles. That day's work proved that the old spirit of the battalion, which came back from Ypres last November only 120 strong after their gallant defence, still lives on.
>
> On the Tuesday night (15th) the Battalion moved out to take part in an attack at the most dangerous part of the Ypres salient. Their chief part was to consolidate and hold the trenches about to be taken from the enemy, and go through the trying ordeal of the terrible artillery bombardment by means of which the Germans endeavour to take back the trenches they have lost.
>
> At 2.50 a.m. began the preliminary artillery bombardment by our guns and all agree as to the terribly destructive effect of our shellfire. Then came the attack. The Royal Irish Rifles were not expected to go beyond the second line of German trenches, but the gallant Irish could not be held back and three companies actually reached the third line of German trenches.
>
> Having made a gallant charge they returned in perfect order to the lines they were to hold and there they withstood all day a bombardment

> so terrific that those who have been through the whole campaign say that it was more fierce than anything they had experienced. The losses were numerically great, but the number of slightly wounded was luckily unusually high in comparison with the total number of casualties. The writer spoke with many of the wounded as they came back and was greatly struck by their splendid spirits and enthusiasm.
>
> They streamed down the road to Ypres under shell-fire, carrying all sorts of trophies – German helmets, rifles, automatic pistols, map cases, telescopic sights and last but not least a perfect German machine-gun. They found the Germans taken completely by surprise and completely panic-stricken. They were contemptuous of the Germans' 'cowardice', not so much because they gave themselves up as prisoners, but because they cringed down with joined hands and whined out, 'Gude English' and no longer 'Gott Strafe England'.
>
> The next night the battalion, having handed over the captured trenches to another regiment, returned to their camp, much reduced in numbers indeed, but with new courage.

In July 1917 he was seconded for service in the King's African Rifles in East Africa where he soon acquired a good working knowledge of Ki-Swahili but suffered many hardships fighting the Germans. After the war he volunteered for service in Somaliland, a place he had tried to get to in his first days of soldiering. However, he died of cerebral malaria before taking up the posting. He had been twice mentioned in dispatches, 1 January 1916 and 5 June 1919.

Charles Wakefield is listed in the Commonwealth War Graves Commission Debt of Honour Register with the rank of major. In 1921 the then vicar gave a plot in St Giles' Churchyard for his Stoke Poges memorial. For a few years after the war it was the custom each November to publish in the Parish Magazine a list of all the fallen in the war. Wakefield's name was added to this list.

Perhaps we should allow Pte Edward Elderfield to record the final tribute. On hearing that Wakefield had been wounded in 1915, he wished him well in a letter from the front and wrote, 'It is a great honour for one of our villagers to rise from the ranks.'

EPILOGUE

Chapter Eight

The Homecoming and the War Memorial

As early as January 1916 consideration was being given to the provision of a war memorial. By this time six men had died and there was a call for individual memorial tablets. The vicar, churchwardens and sidesmen considered that there should be one joint memorial to which not only relatives of fallen soldiers but friends and the entire parish could contribute. One joint memorial to which all parishioners could contribute would symbolise the unity of feeling that the war had evoked.

By September 1917, 27 men had died and the vicar was having more requests for private memorials in the church. It was decided to consider various proposals for a memorial, one of which was for the restoration of the Hastings Chapel and the erection of a marble tablet in the chapel containing the names of all those who had given their lives. A fund was established and a Stoke Poges War Memorial Account was opened. Algernon Gilliat offered £50 if a joint memorial in the church was agreed upon.

The Bishop of Oxford asked parishes to postpone until after the war the erection of memorials and stressed the need to persuade rich and poor to combine in one corporate memorial. Envisaging many individual memorials being erected in churches, he warned that 'the beauty of our old churches is at stake'.

120 *Henry Allhusen of Stoke Court.*

121 *Algernon Gilliat.*

122 *Canon Arthur Barnett, Vicar of Stoke Poges 1912-26.*

123 *Charles Gilliat (Chairman of the Parish Council 1913-15), son of Algernon.*

In June 1918 a Special Parish Meeting was held in the local school and a representative committee was set up to consider the form and site of a memorial or memorials to be erected. The committee consisted of ten members, chaired by the chairman of the parish council, Mr Howard Henry Howard-Vyse. Four of the members were fathers of men who had died. These were Mr John Bowen who had lost his two sons Martin and Harold; Mr Ernest Shepherd whose 18-year-old son had died in the *Vanguard* explosion; Mr George Gutteridge six of whose sons served, one of whom, Walter, had lost his life, and Mr James Birch who lost two of his sons, Arthur and William. The remaining members were Canon Barnett, Mr Henry Allhusen, Dr Morriston-Davies, Mr Charles Gilliat and Mrs F. Hartley.

The Committee set out to consider all the suggestions it had received. Further suggestions were welcomed. The objective was to bring about a unanimous decision and, it was said, there was no reason why there should not be two memorials, one in the church listing the names of the fallen and another of a more secular character on a suitable site.

With the war at an end and soldiers returning, Canon Barnett again referred to the subject in the February 1919 Parish Magazine when he wrote:

> The Committee appointed to recommend the form the Memorial should take, may be expected at an early date to lay its report before a Parish Meeting. It will then be for such a Meeting to accept, modify or reject the suggestions made.

124 *James Birch and Ellen Birch.*

The large majority of those who have lost relatives in the war are anxious that part, at all events, of the money collected should be spent in some memorial in our Church. It seems natural it should be so, for it is through the teaching of Christ that our faith in the spiritual world has been quickened, and hence about the Church for centuries the memorials of our dead have been gathered.

In the case of the Stoke Poges Church there is, however, a secondary, yet important, reason why a memorial should find a place within its walls. Owing to its association with Gray's Elegy and the Penn family, our Church has become each year the place of pilgrimage for some 5,000 English-speaking people from beyond the seas. Naturally these visitors from Canada, Australia, New Zealand, South Africa and the United States will expect to find, in what is perhaps the best-known parish church in the Empire, a fitting memorial to that gallant band of forty men who, from this small village, have given their lives for their King and Country.

One other reason has, we think, prompted this wish for some memorial in the Church. Owing to our climate a list of names does not long remain legible out of doors, and the Church is the only building in the parish where the care of any memorial is assured by custom and by law.

The fact that a consensus of opinion seems in favour of some memorial in the Church does not, of course, exclude any second memorial to our men; they are worthy of all, and more than all, that we can do to perpetuate their memory. We deprecate any sense of rivalry between a Church memorial and one of a more secular character, for we feel that each is complementary to the other.

What we would suggest is, that the Parish Meeting might make it known that there will be two memorials, one in the Church, the other of a more secular character. The large majority of subscribers would probably wish to give to both, and would divide their subscriptions in accordance with their predilections; the rest would give to one or to the other as they thought well. This would effectively eliminate every trace of rivalry, for both memorials would be part of a JOINT scheme, and neither would have spent on it more than was directly contributed to that particular object.

125 *Stoke Poges ex-servicemen photographed in March 1919 in front of Gray's Monument.*

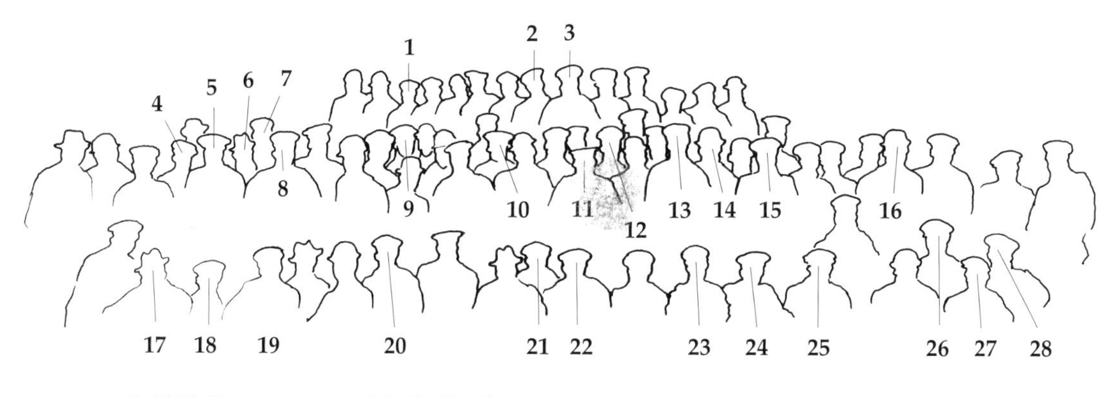

1 G.H. Dorsett	8 R.G. Harding	15 'Todger' Penn	22 Arthur Overshott
2 H. Bunby	9 Bill Day	16 Ted Dunton	23 Bryant
3 W. Glennerster	10 L.J. Kilby	17 Bert Butler	24 Elderfield
4 'Kruger' Gale	11 H. Harding	18 Charles Webb	25 Fred Spring
5 Ernie Gutteridge	12 Albert Baldwin	19 Bill Gutteridge	26 W. Gedge
6 Fred Hartley	13 R. Howard-Vyse	20 Reuben Tarrant	27 Harry Hazell
7 Alf Gutteridge	14 Ted Elderfield	21 Percy Plumridge	28 F.E. Betts

126 *Richard Howard-Vyse of Stoke Place (knighted in 1935).*

In August 1919 the returned soldiers and sailors were invited to a supper in a huge marquee with entertainment afterwards in the Village Hall. At this event Colonel Richard Howard-Vyse, proposing the toast to the hosts, said that though soldiering was his life's work he felt the hatefulness of war and indeed thankful it was all over. Corporal Alistair Cripps, of Fern Hill, Uxbridge Road, who had served in the Royal Engineers, added his thanks. After the supper each of the guests was presented with a walking stick on the silver mounting of which the date and name was later engraved.

At about this time a second parish meeting agreed to the erection in the chancel of St Giles of a tablet bearing the names of 46 men. It also agreed that a recreation ground, with a memorial stone thereon, should be provided on the Stoke Common Fuel Allotment or elsewhere.

127 *Memorial Tablet in St Giles' Church.*

128 *Stoke Poges vicarage, built 1802-4 and designed by James Wyatt.*

129 *The bronze plaque inscribed 'Arthur William Plumridge'.*

The Memorial Tablet of Hoptonwood Stone, designed and executed by Sir Ernest George and Mr Basil Gotto, was placed on the north wall of the chancel. This was considered one of the best positions in the church and it was made possible by Howard Henry Howard-Vyse who arranged for the removal from that position of a monument to one of his relatives. The cost of the memorial was £350 and the final list contained 48 names. Unfortunately, the tablet contains three errors, despite the efforts made to ensure that the details were correct. Henry Dancer's regiment is shown as the Royal Berkshire instead of the Oxford and Bucks Light Infantry; the initials of Private Cutting are shown as V.F. instead of W.F.; and, more seriously, T.Collison was changed to T.Collinson. Nevertheless, the erection of the memorial inside the church and the excellence of the design are a credit to the committee who made the decisions.

The unveiling by the Dean of Windsor, Dr Baillie, took place at a service on Sunday afternoon, 4 January 1920. The body of the church was reserved for the relatives of the departed on one side, and the members of the Demobilised Federation, the forerunner of the Royal British Legion, on the other side. The latter had marched from their headquarters in Stoke Road with their banner and were met by Colonel Richard Howard-Vyse, CMG, DSO. There was not an empty seat in the church and many had to stand. Every relative was presented with a framed photograph of the tablet.

Nationally, a memorial in the form of a bronze plaque was sent to the closest relative of every man and woman killed in the Great War. It carries the inscription 'He [She] died for Freedom and Honour' and the name of the individual. It was sent with a scroll accompanied by a letter from the King. Some 1,150,000 plaques and scrolls were sent to relatives.

Appendix

The following is the final monthly list published in March 1919 showing the names of Parishoners of Stoke Poges serving their country in the Navy, Army, and Territorial Forces.

OFFICERS.

*†nLt.-Col. F. Allhusen, D.S.O., C.M.G., Forestry Directorate, G. H.Q., France
Capt. H. Birdwood, Midsex. R., Larchmoor
*Lieut. A. W. L. Bisset, H M.S. "Iron Duke"
*Eng.Lieut.Comdr.D.Bowen,H.M.S. "Wakeful"
**nCapt. M. Bowen*, M.C., Bucks Batt. O & B.L.I. *wounded* 1916, *killed Oct.* 9*th*, 1917
n*Temp. Major J. Bowen, D.A.D. Ry. Transport,
n**Lieut. H. T. Bowen*, Can. Res. Batt., Appletons, *wounded 1916, killed Jan.* 2*nd*, 1918
n*Capt. C. K. Boyd, Motor Transport, A.S.C.
*Capt. G. Catherall, R.A.F., Stoke Common
n**2 Lieut. W. G. T. Clifton*, R.A.F., *wounded 1915, 1917, killed March* 31*st*, *1917*
*2 Lieut. W. R. Felts, M.T. A S C., Stoke Park
**Capt. C. E. Hanbury*, Irish Gds., *twice wounded 1916, killed Oct. 9th*, 1917
*Brig.-Gen. R. Howard-Vyse, C,M.G., D.S.O., Desert Mounted Corps, E.E.F.
n**Capt. L. A. Judd*, H.L.I., *wounded 1915*
d**2 Lieut. W. J. Newberry*, R. West Kent Regt. Farnham Road, *wounded* 1917, *invalided* 1918
n*Lieut. K.M. Oppenheimer, Indian Army Reserve
*n 2 Lieut. H. M. Parry, K.R.R.C., att. S. Lancs.
n2 Lieut. N. E. Parry, Ghurkas, Indian Army
**Capt. Charles Wakefield*, East African Rifles, *wounded 1915*
**Capt. G. Walmsley*, K.R.R.C., *wounded 1915*
**Lieut. A. Walmsley*, M.C., R. Welsh Fusiliers, *wounded 1914, 1915*
**2 Lieut. J. A. Whareham*, Durham L.I., Gladstone Cottages, *wounded 1916*
*Thomas G. Pridden, Gunner, H.M.S. Implacable

OTHER RANKS & RATINGS.

n*Ablett, Pte. H., 2 O. & B.L.I.
*nAlbrow, Pte. E. C., City of London, 21, Farnham Road
**Albrow, Pte. H.*,M.T., A.S.C., 16, Farnham Road, *killed 27th April*, 1918
Albrow, Pte. A. G., Bedford Regt,, Stoke Common
**nAlden, Sergt. A.*, Lab. Batt. Devon Regt., 2, Stoke Park Cottages, *wounded* 1917
n**Alsford, Corpl. R.*, Middx. Regt.,Wexham Street *killed*
n*Alsford, Pte. F., Wexham Street
*Andrews, Lce.-Cpl.A.,WarwickRegt.,Clevehurst
nAsh, Trooper D., Life Guards, Stoke Park
*Ashton, Pte. C., O. & B.L.I.
d**Bacon, Pte. B.*, Yorks L.I., The Schoolhouse, *wounded* 1917
**nBaldwin, Pte. A. E.*, Bucks T., West End, *wounded 1916*
*nBaldwin, Pte. U. E., Ches. Res., West End
**Ball, Pte. J.*, G.G., Bells' Hill, *wounded*
d**nBanister, Cpl. Herbert*, Duke of Cornwall's L.I., Uxbridge Road, *wounded 1915, 1917*
*nBanister, Pte. John, M.T., A.S.C., Uxbridge Rd.
n*Banister, Pte.A., M.A.C., A.S.C., Uxbridge Rd.
*Banister, Pte. W., T.R.B., Uxbridge Road
*Banister, Pte. W., 52nd Royal Fusiliers
nBailey, Air Mec. A. C., R.N.A.S., Stoke Green
*Bass, Pte. P. J., M.T., A.S.C., Hill House
n*Bassett, Pte. E., M.T., A.S.C., Wexham Street
**nBateman, John*, R.N., Bells' Hill, *killed Feb. 2nd* 1918
**Bateman, Lce.-Cpl. W. E.*, O. & B.L.I., Wexham Street, *wounded* 1918
n*Batten, Sergt -Major. Ry.-Operating Div., R.E.
**Baylis, Pte. G.*, O. & O.L.I., Vine Cottages, *prisoner* 1918
n*Beach, Driver William, A.S.C., Wexham St.
*Beasley, Sig. H., M.M., 9 Fusiliers, School Lane
*Bennett, A. E., R.N , 5, Jardine Cottages
dn*Betts, Pte. F. E., M.G.C., Bucks, 11 Farnham Road
**Betts, Pte. A.*, Res. Battn. O. & B.L.I., Uxbridge Road, *wounded and a prisoner March 23rd*, 1918
Biggs, Gnr. R. J., R.F.A., Wexham Street
n**Birch, Pte W. J.*, O. & B.L.I., Bells' Hill, *killed August, 1917*
n**Birch, Pte. A. J.*, M. Gun C., Bells' Hill, *killed Sept, 16th, 1916*
nBirch, Pte. A. W., Bells' Hill
Blackwood, Pte. J., R.M.L.C., Sefton Pk. Gardens
dn**Boon, Corpl. A.*, Rifle Bde., Sefton Pk., *wounded 1916*
n*Bottle, L.-Cpl. A., O & B.L.I., Pionrs.
dn**Bowen, L.-Cpl. S. T.*, Glos. Regt., *wounded 1914*
n*Brock, Corpl. A., M.M. Police, Wexham Street
dn**Brock, Pte. R.*, Essex R.,Wexham Street,*wounded*
*Brock, Spr. H., R.E.. Wexham Street
*Brown,W.T,,Leading Stoker, H.M.S. "Vernon," Farnham Road
n*Brown, Pte. J. W., A.S.C., Uxbridge Road
n*Brown, Pte.H.H., M.T., A.S.C., Sefton Cottages
nBryant, Pte. C., R.A.M.C., South Hill Cottages
nBryant, Pte. A., A.S.C., South Hill Cottages
n*Bryant, Pte. G., Bucks, South Hill Cottages
**Bunby, Pte. A. G.*, Bedfords, 20, Farnham Road, *missing, believed killed in action, May 5th*, 1915
nBunby, Pte. R., R.A.M.C., 20, Farnham Road

*nBunby, Lce.-Cpl E. W., R.W. Sur., 20, Farnham Road
Bunby, Pte. H., 6, Farnham Road
**Burgess, Pte. J.*, Norfolks, Bells' Hill, *wounded 1914*
n*Burgess, Dvr. V. R., M.T., A.S.C., Bells' Hill
dnBurgess, 1st A.M. B., R.A.F., Bells' Hill
*nBurgess Pte. R., Worcest. Regt., Uxbridge Road
*n*Burgess, Pte. A. W. J.*, Bucks Batt., Uxbridge Rd., *wounded* 1916, 1917, *prisoner, March* 1918
dnBurgess, Sapper G., R.E., Holly Bush Hill
**Burrows, Qmr.-Sgt. E. F.*, D.C.M., 2 R. Berks, *killed August 16th, 1917*
dn**Butler, Pte. J.A.*, Glos., Bells' Hill, *wounded 1915, 1916, prisoner March 23rd*, 1918
n*Butler, Pte. R., R. Fus., Uxbridge Road
dn**Butler, Pte. E.*, Glos., Uxbridge Road, *wounded 1917*
nButler, Pte. O., Bucks Terr., Uxbridge Road
n**Butler, Pte. F. W.*, Durham L.I., *wounded* 1916
n*Bylett Pte. A., M.T., A.S.C., Stoke Common
Clark, E., R.A.F., Stoke Wood Cottages, *died Oct. 20th*, 1918.
*Clark, Pte. J. C., Devon R., 3, Jardine Cottages
n*Clayton, Corpl. H. J., A.S.C., Bells' Hill
n**Clifton. Pte. R.*, Manch. Regt.. The Bungalow, *killed Aug. 21st*, 1918
**Clinch, Pte. G.*, London R., Hockley Hill, *died Oct. 28th*, 1918
*Cook, Bomb. E. J., R.G.A, The Post Office
*n*Cowell, Pte. R.*, Coldstream G., Stoke Green, *twice wounded 1915, killed July 23rd*, 1918
n*Cripps, Sapper A. B., R.E., Uxbridge Road
n*Crowe, Pte. T., M.T., A.S.C., Larchmoor
*nCull, Pte. A. J., R.W. Kent, Sefton Park Cottages, missing Oct. 26th, 1917
*n*Dancer, Pte. H. J.*, Bells' Hill, *killed May, 1917*
**Davies, A. E., Seaman, Uxbridge Road
*Davis, Pte. Geo., O. & B.L.I., Roger's Lane
nDavis, Pte. T. W., R.E., Bells' Hill
Dawson, Pte. W.J., 1st A.M., R.A.F., Green Lane
**Day, Pte. W.*, C. Gds., Bells' Hill, *wounded* 1918
*Dean, Bombr. W., Batt., R.F.A.
nDean, Pte. E. J., R.G.A., Wexham Street
n**Didcock, Pte. G.*, R. Fus., Wexham Street, *wounded Dec.* 1917, *died in France July* 1918
nDidcock, Pte. C., R.F.C., Wexham Street
n**Dorsett, Sergt. Jas.*, Bucks Batt., Farnham Road, *wounded 1917*
*nDorsett, Pte. G.H., O. & B.L.I., 10, Farnham Rd.
n*Dunton, Gnr. J. A., R.G.A., 1, Southill Cottages
n*Dunton, Pte. W. E., O. & B.L.I., West End
Edwards, Pte. W., R. Berks Regt., Labour Batt., Holly Bush Hill
**Elderfield, Pte. E.*, O. & B.L.I., Wexham St., *wounded 1915, invalided*
n*Elderfield, Driver Hy., A.S.C., Wexham Street
*†nElderfield, Coy. Q.M.-Sergt. Alfred, A.S.C., Wexham Street
n*Elderfield, Driv. J. O., A.S.C., Holly Bush Hill
n*Enstone, Driv. H., R.F.A., South Hill Cottages
*†*Evans, Sergt. J.*, R. Berks, Hockley Hole, *killed July 1st, 1916*
*n*Evered, Sapper Geo. E.*, R.E., Wexham Street, *invalided, died Oct. 25th*, 1918
*Field, Bombr. R., R.F.A., Wexham Street
*nField, Pte. G. J., Bucks Terr.
*†nFinch, L.-Cpl. J., Mil. Police, West End

n**Fleet, Pte. A.*, S. Wales Bdrs., Holly Bush Hill, *wounded 1915, invalided*
Fleet, A., Boy Telegraphist, H.M.S. Lion, Holly Bush Hill
n**Fleet, Pte. H.*, Wexham Street, *missing May 9th, 1917*
*Flitton, Pte. W., Hussars, Stoke Place Farm
*nFlitton, Sgt. G. A., M.T., A.S.C., Stoke Pl. Farm
*Freeman, Pte. H. H. J., O. & B.L.I., School Lane
nFrith, Pte. L., A.S.C., Stoke Court Cottages
*nFry, Pte. J., O. & B.L.I.
*nGale, Pte. B., Bucks Batt., Bells' Hill
**Gale, Sergt. W.*, Berks Regt., West End, *wounded 1914, killed March 12th, 1917*
*Gale, O.S., A., R.N., West End
d*†nGedge, Pnr. C. R., R.E., Sefton Cottages
*nGedge, Gnr. W., R.G.A., West End
*n*Gibbons, Sergt.-Major J. F.*, M.M., Austln. Bn., Wexham Street, *wounded 1914, 1915*
Gibbons, Pte. A., T.R. Battn., Wexham Street
*nGlennerster, Pte. W., Farnham Road
**Grace, Pte. E.*, R.E., Stoke Grn., *wounded 1914, 1917*
n*Grant, Pte. A.S., Rex Cottages
*nGroves, Cpl. E., R. Fusiliers, Wexham Street
*nGroves, Pte. F. A., M.T., A.S.C., Wexham Street
**Gutteridge, L.-Cpl. H.*, M.F.P., Bells' Hill, *wounded 1914*
**Gutteridge, Sergt. W.*, attd. Mnstrs., Bells' Hill, *wounded 1915, killed in action Oct 3rd, 1916*
*n*Gutteridge, L.-Cpl. Alfred*, Suss. Yeo., Bells' Hill, *wounded 1916*
n**Gutteridge, Pte. E.*, Hants Regt., Bells' Hill, *wounded, invalided 1915.*
†nGutteridge, Gnr. G. W., R.G.A., Wexham Street
n**Gutteridge, Pte. A.*, M.M., O. & B.L.I., Bells' Hill, *wounded 1916*
n**Gutteridge, Gnr. G. T.*, R.F.A., 14, Farnham Road, *wounded 1916*
Gutteridge, Gnr. W. J., Res. Batt. R.F.A. 14, Farnham Road
*n*Hagger, Pte. S.*, Fus., Farnham Rd., *prisoner*
**Hamilton, Pte. L. W.*, R. E. Kent Mounted Rifles, Larchmoor, *wounded 1915*
n**Hammond, L.-Cpl. H.*, O. & B.L.I., *died of wounds Oct. 3rd, 1915*
†n**Hancock, Pte. E.*, O. & B.L.I., Wexham St., *invalided* 1918
**Harding, Rifleman J.*, R.B., Stoke Grn., *wounded* 1916, 1917
n*Harding, Sgt. R.G., O.&B.Pioneers, Stoke Grn.
*Harding, H., R.N.R., A.B., R.N.C., VineCottages
*n*Hare, Pte. R. H.*, O & B.L.I., West End, *wounded* 1916
nHarris, Cpl. F. J., Batt. Devon Regt., Framewood
Harris, Spr. S. F., R.E., Stoke Cottage
Harris, Pte. F. H., Remounts, Stoke Place
dn*Hartley, Sgt. F., San. Corps., R.A.M.C., Stoke Green
Hartley, Pte., Stoke Green
Hawkes, Pte. A., R.A.F., Parochial Room
**Hazell, Lce.-Cpl. G.H.*, Wilts Regt., Uxbridge Road, *wounded* 1915, 1916
dn**Hazell, Pte. H.*, Bucks Terr., Uxbridge Rd., *wounded* 1916
d**Hay, Sgt. J.S.*, R. Fus., Wexham St., *thrice wounded*
*Healy, Cpl. R. W., R.F.A., Wexham Street

*d**n*†*Herbert, Corpl. J.*, R.E., Bells' Hill, *wounded* 1916
***n*Hinge, Pte. H. W., R.A.M.C., 7, Uxbridge Road
*†Holdship, Pte. H., O. & B.L.I., Farnham Road
*n**Howse, Pte. F., M.T., A.S.C., School Lane
*Howse, Lce.-Cpl. B., R.G.A., School Lane
*d***Hucker, Tpr. J.*, L.G., Wexham Street, *prisoner*
*n*Hucker, Pte. A., H.L.I., Wexham Street
Hucker, Rfm. C., London Regt., Wexham Street
*Hutchins, Sapper E. W., R.E.
*n***Humphries, Pte. E.*, Glos., Bells' Hill, *killed April 4th*, 1918
*n**Hughes, Sapper H., R.E., Stoke Green
*n*Hughes, Gnr. C. N., R.G.A., 5, Gladstone Villas
*d***Isbell, Pte. A. E.*, O.&.B.L.I., Uxbridge Rd., *wounded* 1915, *invalided* 1918
***n*Isbell, L.-Cpl. G., Essex Regt., Uxbridge Road
*n***James, Spr. A.*, R.E., Wexham Street, *invalided Dec., 1916, died June 5th, 1917*
*d**Jennings, Pte. J. M.T., A.S.C., Stoke Pk. Grdns.
*d***n*Johnson, L.-Corpl. A., O & B.L.I.Terr., Duffield Cottage
Johnson, Pte. C. J., Sth. A. Scot., Stoke Green, *killed Oct. 17th*, 1918
*n***Jolley, Pte. R.*, Bucks Batt., 1, Farnham Road, *wounded* 1916, 1917
*Jordan, Pte. A., Stoke Park
Kilby, Spr. L. J., R.E., School Lane
*†*King, Sergt. A. G.*, R.M.L.I., Rose Cottages, *killed March 11th, 1915.*
*n***King, Sergt. F. J.* O. & B.L.I., Stoke Place, *missing May 9th, 1917*
*n*King, Pte. A., Berkshire Regiment
*King, Gnr. G. H., R.G.A., Stoke Green
*n**Knight, Pte. P., M.T., A.S.C., Stoke Court
†*n**Knight, Sgt. W., Scots Guards, Rogers Lane
*n*Lane, Pte. W. P. V., A.O. Corps, Bells' Hill
*Larking, Gnr. T. R.G.A., Wexham Street
*Lavington, Pte. F., A.S.C., Framewood
*Lawrence, Sergt. W., Hants Regt., Rogers Lane
**Lawrence, Pte. A. J.*, R.N.D., Rogers Lane, *killed Sept. 28th*, 1918
**Leslie, Sergt. F.*, D.C.M., Berks Regt., Stoke Common, *wounded* 1917
*Loe, Chief Petty Officer, R.N.R., Stoke Park
Lovejoy, 3rd A.M. L. H., R.F.C., 6, Uxbridge Road
***n**Lovejoy, Drvr. A. J.*, A.S.C., 6, Uxbridge Road, *wounded* 1914
†*n**Lowe, Bomb. A.E., M.M., R.G.A., Wexham St
**Mayne, Pte. William*, O. & B.L.I., Stoke Park, *died of wounds Sept. 22nd, 1914*
***n**Margetts, Cpl. F.*, Rifle Bde., Hedgerley Road, *died of wounds Dec. 15th, 1915*
***n*Marshall, Pte. E. C., D.Cornwall, Hedgerley Rd.
*MacLean, Cpl. A., Grenadier Gds., Stoke Park
*n***Measday, Pte. F.*, King's Liv. Regt., Sefton Cots., *wounded* 1916
***n**Measday, Sergt. S.*, S. Irish Horse, Sefton Cots., *killed Dec. 30th*, 1917
***n**Measday, Pte. W.*, S. Staffs. Regt., Sefton Cottages, *killed July 1st, 1917*
*n*Mitchell, Corpl. A., O.&B.L.I., Wexham Street
***n**Mitchell, Cpl. H. F.*, E. Sur., Holly Bush Hill, *died of wounds April 25th, 1917*
*n**Moore, L.-Cpl. C., M.M., R.E., Wexham Street
Mortimer, Pte. M. C., Res. Batt. D.C.L.I., Wexham Wood
*n**Mortlock, H., Telegraphist, R.N., Sefton Cots.
*n*Nancollis, Pte. W., Cheshires, Stoke Park
***n*Nason, Cpl. T., O. & B.L.I., Stoke Court
†*n***Newns, Sgt. H.*, S. Staffs. R., Stoke Grn., *wounded* 1915, 1916, *killed Nov. 13th*, 1916
*n**Nicholls, Pte. D. H. R., M.T., A.S.C.
*n*Nicholls, Pte. D., M.M., R.A.M.C., Stoke Park
*d***Overshott, Corpl. W.*, London Regt., 4, South Hill Cottages, *wounded* 1915
***n*Overshott, Pte. A., Royal Berks, Bells' Hill
***n**Palmer, Pte. H.*, R.W. Surrey Regt., *wounded*
**Pargeter, Coy. Qrmstr.-Sgt. W.*, R. Scots, Stoke Common, *wounded* 1914
**Pargeter, L.-Cpl. F.*, Royal Scots, Stoke Common, *wounded* 1914
*Pargeter, Joseph R.N., Stoke Common
*d**†*Parker, Spr. C. M.*, R.E., Holly Bush Hill
*n***Payne, Cpl. F.*, C Batt., Bde., R.F.A., *wounded* 1918
d†*Penn, Pte. E.*, Middlesex, Wexham Street, reserve
*n***Plumridge, Corpl. P.*, Bucks Battn., Farnham Road, *thrice wounded*
***n**Plumridge, Pte. A. W.*, Mac. G.C. Bucks Batt., 2, Farnham Road, *killed in action Nov. 1, 1916*
*n*Poolman, Pte. P., A.S.C., Stoke Common
*n*Poolman, Pte, G., O. & B.L.I., Stoke Common
Powell, Pte. J. H., R.A.F., Wexham Street
Powney, Pte. F., R.M.L.I., Stoke Common
*Pridden, Pte. H., R.A.M.C., Baylis House
***n**Pullen, Dvr. J. H.*, D.A.C., R.F.A., *killed April 30th*, 1918
*†*Reynolds, Cpl. F. J.*, Gren. Gds., *died of wound April 21st, 1916*
*n*Richards, Gnr. G., R.F.A., Stoke Green
***n**Robinson, Pte. C. J.*, M.G. Coy., Bucks, Uxbridge Road, *killed*
**Rogers, Pte. L.*, R. Fus., Fulmer Grange Lodge, *prisoner*
**Rogers, Cpl. W.*, R. Fus., Fulmer Grange Lodge, *killed in action Oct. 9th, 1916*
*n*Rooke, Pte. T., R.G.A., 8, Farnham Road
***n*Savin, Drvr. J., M.T., A.S.C., 3, South HillCots,
***n**Sayers, Pte E.*, Worcester Regt., Stoke Common. *wounded* 1917
*Selfe, Edward, A.B., R.N., Hockley Hole
*n**Sharp, Tpr. E., Life Guards, Sefton Park
**Shepherd, E.*, R.N. Telegraphist, Lion Lodge, *killed July 12th, 1917*
*n***Skues, Corpl. H.*, O. & B.L.I., Stoke Park, *killed August 24th, 1916*
Sleath, Spr. A. P., R.E., Wexham Street
Smith, Pte. A., Gladstone Villas
*d***n**Spring, Pte. F.*, O. & B.L.I., StokeGreen, *wounded* 1917
***n**Stahr, Pte. R.*, Gloucester Regt., Stoke Common, *killed Nov. 8th, 1915*
*n***Stallwood, Pte. R. F.*, Wilts, Sefton Pk., *wounded*
*n**Staples, Pte. W., Wilts Regt., Duffield
*Staples, Corpl. E., R.E., Stoke Park
*n*Steptoe, Pte. H. T., A.S.C., Holly Bush Hill
*d*Stephens, Pte. H., Bedford Regt., Uxbridge Rd.
†*n**Swabey, Dvr. W., Batt., R.F.A., Stoke Green
*Tansley, Pte. L. C., R. Marines, Sefton Cottages

d*nTarrant, Spr. R., R. Engineers, Uxbridge Road
Tarrant, Pte. J., C.G., Uxbridge Road
*Tarry, Drvr. W., Hants Regt., School Lane
*Tarry, Pte. F., Berks Regt., School Lane
*Tarry, Pte., Hants Regt., School Lane
*Thompson, Pte. R., O. & B.L.I., Sefton Cots.
n*Topple, Pte. T., M.T., R.E., Stoke Court
*nTimms, Cpl. W. A., M.G.C., Holly Bush Hill
*nTimms, Bombr. E. H., R.G.A., Holly Bush Hill
nTimms, Cpl. F., Berks R., Holly Bush Hill, *wounded* 1917
dTindell, Pte. L., West End, *invalided*
**Trinder, Pte. T.*, Wexham Street, *killed May, 1917*
n*Turner, Corpl. F., R.E., 4, Hockley Hole
*d†n*Turner, Pte. S.*, A. Vet. Corps., Conniston Cots.
nTurner, Pte. L., R.A.M.C., Wexham St.
nVallis, Sergt. H., R.E., Stoke Green
nVallis, Pte. R. B., A.Vet.C., Stoke Green
n*Vine, Pte. E., Motor Transport, Framewood
n*Wallis, Pte. G., Glos. Regt., Stoke Court
d*Way, Cpl. S., M.M., Tank Corps
Waterman, Pte. C. H., R.G.A., Hockley Hole
*nWard, Cpl. W., 1 Air Mech. R.A.F., West End
*n*Ware, Pte. E.*, O. & B.L.I., Wexham St., *wounded* 1915
**Webb, Sergt. C. W.*, M.M., Berks Regt., 19, Farnham Road, *five times wounded*
n†Webb, Pte. H., R.F.A., Hockley Hole
Webb, Pte. F., Q.W.S., Hockley Hole
*Webb, A. C. G., 2 A.M., R.A.F., Stoke Place Farm
†n*Werrell, Cpl. A., R.F.A., M, Stoke Green
n*Werrell, S-Smith H., R.F.A., Stoke Green
d*nWheeler, Dvr. J., Sth. Lancs. Transport, Holly Bush Hill
nWhent, Pte. W. F., Qn. Vic. Rifles, West End
Whitehead, Pte. H. J. Queen's Regt., Clevehurst
*Whent, F., R.N., H.M.S. Inconstant, West End
nWhittick, Pte. F. A., Army Veterinary Corps
Winchcombe, Pte. W. G., Devon Regt., Wexham Street
*nWinter, L.-Cpl. F., Worc. Regt., Stoke Common
*nYeatman, Cpl. W., S. Irish Horse, Pond Cottage
d*nYeatman, Pte. J., A.S.C., Pond Cottage

———

Women Serving.

W. Ward, R. Air Force

n Volunteered since outbreak of War
* Has been or is on active service
† Had left the Service but re-joined
d Demobilized

There may be mistakes or omissions in the above list. Please send a post-card with corrections or additions to Canon A. T. Barnett, The Vicarage, before the 15th of each month. He would be glad to have also any news of those in the list for inclusion in this Magazine. Any letters, &c , lent for this purpose would be treated with the greatest care and returned without delay

War Diaries and Other Documents, at the National Archives, Kew

Albrow, H.E., 14th Bt. Duke of Cornwall's Light Infantry, WO95/4693
Alsford, R.T., 13th Bt. Middlesex Regiment, WO95/2219
Bateman, L.J., Royal Navy, ADM 8514/48
Birch, A.J., 21st Bt. 64th Company, Machine Gun Corps, WO 95/2162
Birch, W.J., 1/4th Bt. Oxford & Bucks Light Infantry, WO 3291/1861
Bunby, A.G., 1st Bt. Bedfordshire Regiment, WO95/1570
Clifton, R.T.H., 1/9th Manchester Regiment, WO95/2660
Collison, T.C., M.T.'G', Special Company, A.S.C., WO95/242
Cowell, R., 4th Bt. Coldstream Guards, WO95/1206
Cull, A.J., 1st Bt. Royal West Kent Regiment, WO95/1555
Cutting, W.F., 1st Bt. South Staffordshire Regiment, WO95/1670
Dancer, H.J., 7th Bt. Oxford & Bucks Light Infantry, WO329/1363
Evans, J., 2nd Bt. Royal Berkshire Regiment, WO95/1729
Fleet, H.G., 7th Bt. Oxford & Bucks Light Infantry, WO329/1364
Gutteridge, W., 6th Bt. Royal Munster Fusiliers, WO95/4837
Hammond, H., 5th Bt. Oxford & Bucks Light Infantry, WO95/1365, WO329/1365
Hanbury, C.E.R., 2nd Bt. Irish Guards, WO95/1220
Humphries, E., 10th Bt. Gloucestershire Regiment, WO95/1265
King, F.J., 7th Bt. Oxford & Bucks Light Infantry, WO329/1367
Leslie, G.E., 2/1st Bt. Oxford & Bucks Light Infantry, WO329/1367
Maclean, A., 2nd Bt. Grenadier Guards, WO95/1342
Margetts, F., 7th Bt. Rifle Brigade, WO95/1896
Mayne, W., 2nd Bt. Oxford & Bucks Light Infantry, WO329/1368 & 2461
Measday, S., 3rd Bt. Royal Dublin Fusiliers, WO228/20/207
Measday, W., 1/6th Bt. South Staffordshire Regiment, WO95/2687
Newns, H., 2nd Bt. South Staffordshire Regiment, WO95/1362
Plumridge, A.W., 56th Company Machine Gun Corps, WO95/2082
Reynolds, F.J., 3rd Bt. Grenadiers Guards, WO95/1219
Robinson, C.J., 36th Bt. Machine Gun Corps, WO95/2498
Rogers, W., 9th Bt. Royal Fusiliers, WO95/1857
Shepherd, E.R., Royal Navy, ADM1/8492/153 & ADM137/3681
Skues, H.S., 5th Bt. Oxford & Bucks Light Infantry, WO329/1371
Stahr, R., 5th Bt. Oxford & Bucks Light Infantry, WO95/1265
Trinder, T., 1st Bt. Royal Marines Light Infantry, WO95/3110
Tyson, A.M., Army Service Corps, WO364/4343

DOCUMENTS CONSULTED AT OTHER ARCHIVES

Bowen, H., 2nd Canadian Mounted Rifles, National Archives of Canada
Denteith, T. (6251) 16th Bt. Australian Infantry, National Archives of Australia
Johnson, C.J. (15810) 4th Regiment, South African Infantry, Department of Defence, South Africa

Bibliography

Arthur, Max, *The True Glory: The Royal Navy: 1914-1939 A Narrative History*, Hodder and Stoughton, 1996

Baker, Rodney and Leonard, Alan, *Great Steamers White and Gold – A History of Royal Mail Ships and Services*, Ensign Publications, 1993

Blackman, Dorothy, *Cippenham and Hitcham War Heroes*, Basingstoke Press 1995

Brown, Malcolm, *The Imperial War Museum Book of the Somme*, Pan Books, 1997

Gilbert, Martin, *First World War*, Harper Collins, 1995

Gliddon, Gerald, *When the Barrage Lifts: a topographical history and commentary on the Battle of the Somme 1916*, Gliddon Books, Norwich, Norfolk, 1987

Hickey, Michael, *Gallipoli*, John Murray, 1995

Holmes, Richard, *The Western Front*, BBC Worldwide Ltd, 1999

Jackson, N. Lane ('Pa'), *Sporting Days and Sporting Ways*, Hurst & Blackett, 1932

Johnstone, Tom, *Orange Green & Khaki The Story of The Irish Regiments In The Great War, 1914-18*, Gill and Macmillan, 1992

Kipling, Rudyard, *The Irish Guards in the Great War*, two volumes, Macmillan, London, 1923

Regimental Chronicles of the Oxfordshire and Buckinghamshire Light Infantry for the years 1914/15, 1915/16, 1916/17 and 1917/18

Pears, Randolph, *British Battleships 1892-1957*, Putnam, 1957

Rhodes, Robert James, *Gallipoli*, B.T. Batsford, London, 1965

Robertson, John, *ANZAC and Empire, The Tragedy & Glory of Gallipoli*, Leo Cooper, 1990

Stoke Poges Parish Magazines, 1894 to 1900, 1912 to 1920

Swann, C.B., D.L., Major-General J.C., *The Citizen Soldiers of Buckinghamshire 1795-1926*, published for the Buckinghamshire Territorial Army Association by Hazell, Watson & Viney Ltd.

Tallet, Kyle and Tasker, Trevor, *Gavrelle*, Leo Cooper, 2000

Wakefield, Alan and Moody, Simon, *Under The Devil's Eye Britain's Forgotten Army At Salonika 1915-1918*, Sutton Publishing, 2004

Ward, G. Kingsley and Gibson, Major Edwin, *Courage Remembered*, HMSO, 1989

Westlake, Ray, *British Regiments At Gallipoli*, Leo Cooper, 1996

Wright, Captain P.L., DSO, MC, *The First Buckinghamshire Battalion 1914-1918*, Hazell, Watson & Viney Ltd, 1920

Index

Compiled by Susan Vaughan

Page numbers in **bold** denote illustrations.
The alphabetical list of servicemen on pages 149-52 has not been indexed.

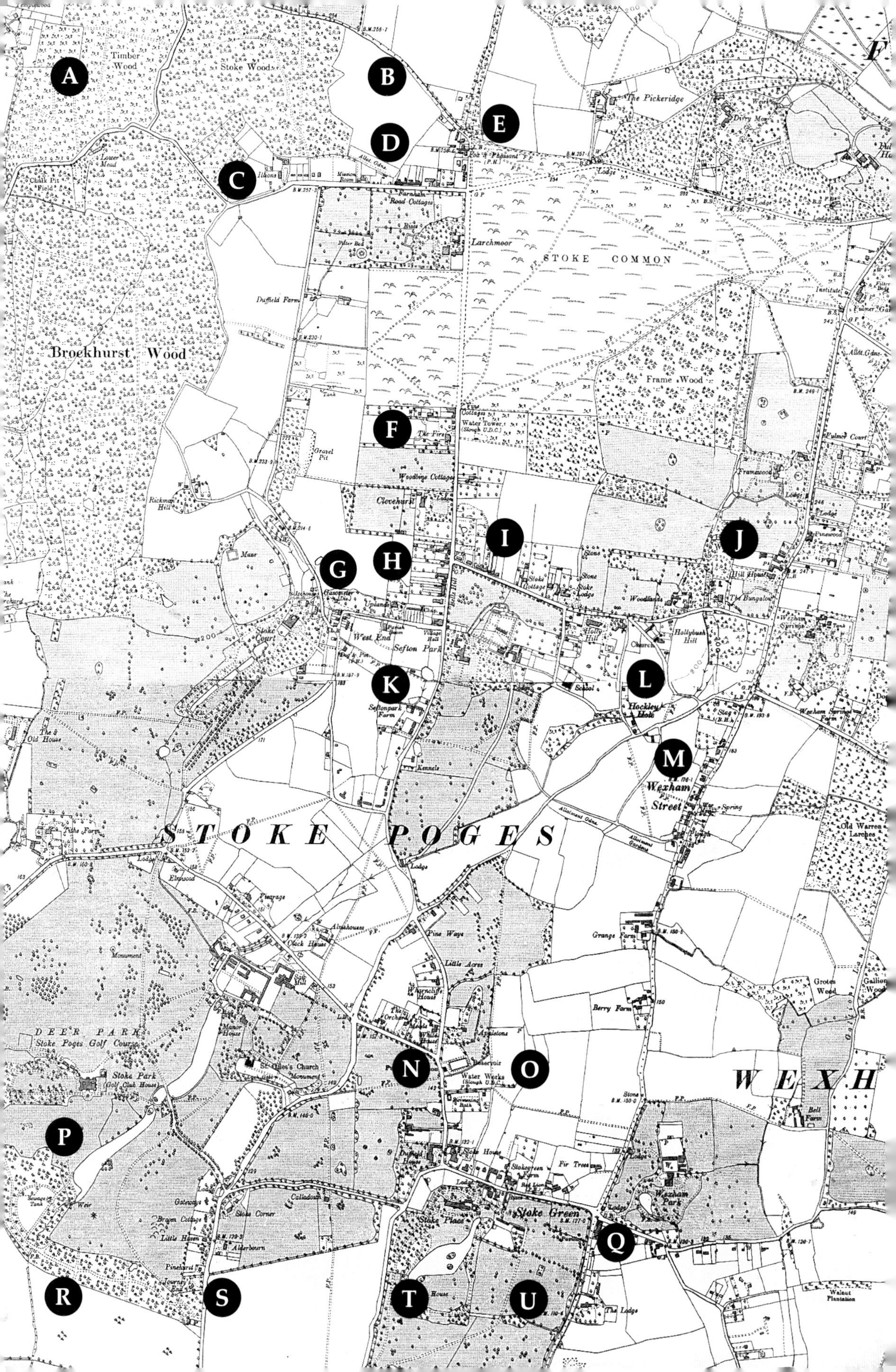

A
B
C
D
E
F
G
H
I
J
K
L
M
N
O
P
Q
R
S
T
U
Timber Wood
Stoke Wood
The Pickeridge
Chalk Pit Field
Lower Mead
Mission Room
Farnham Road Cottages
Larchmoor
STOKE COMMON
Duffield Farm
Brockhurst Wood
Frame Wood
Institute
Fulmer Court
Framewood
Water Tower (Slough U.D.C.)
The Firs
Gravel Pit
Woodbine Cottage
Clevehurst
Rickman Hill
Maze
Gasometer
Uplands
Stoke Court
West End
Sefton Park
Stoke Cottage
Stoke Lodge
Woodlands
Holly Hill
Hollybush Hill
Hill House
The Bungalow
Wexham Springs
School
Hockley Hole
Seftonpark Farm
Kennels
The Old House
Wexham Street
Old Warren Larches
Tithe Farm
STOKE POGES
Lodge
Elmwood
Vicarage
Almshouses
Clock House
Pine Ways
Little Acres
Grange Farm
Berry Farm
Groves Wood
Monument
Wharncliffe House
The Orchard
Appletons
DEER PARK
Stoke Poges Golf Course
Manor House
St. Giles's Church
Stoke Park (Golf Club House)
Reservoir
Water Works (Slough U.D.C.)
WEXH
Bell Farm
Duffield House
Stoke House
Stokegreen Farm
Fir Trees
Stoke Green
Stoke Place
Wexham Park
Gateways
Broom Cottage
Little Haven
Stoke Corner
Alderbourn
Pinehurst
Weir
The Lodge
Walnut Plantation